About the Author

NUSHA HEWAGE IS an IT and business leader with two decades of industry experience in various Fortune 100 companies, in both global and regional capacities. Anusha has specialized in major program/project management, portfolio management, risk management, digital business transformation, organizational management, and change management.

Anusha is passionate about a new way of working which focuses on creating better working environments and developing next-generation leaders. She is focused on people and leadership development through coaching and mentoring.

Anusha has nearly a decade of experience in Agile conducting various Agile transformation programs across a few organizations. She is a Certified Scrum Master, Certified Scaled Program Consultant (SAFe SPC), Agile Certified Practitioner (PMI-ACP), enterprise Agile coach and trainer and a researcher.

Anusha earned a Master's degree from the University of Oxford, United Kingdom.

Contact her at: ahclicks@gmail.com
Subscribe and follow her on social media via:
https://agilebusinessschool.org/

BECOMING A SCRUM MASTER

Everything you should know to be
a GREAT Scrum Master

ANUSHA HEWAGE

Dedication

To My Mother

Contents

Introduction

Bout a decade ago, most people, especially those not
involved in IT, knew nothing about Agile. However, fast-
forward ten years, and almost all organizations and enterprises know a bit about Agile. Agile transformation has in fact begun
in most organizations, but others are unsure about where and how
to start.

Most people who have experience with Agile agree on one
particular thing: it is a better way of working. The scrum master
plays a significant role in Agile transformation by helping the team
work the Agile way, ensuring that the team is well organized and
that each member is always serving the greater good of the team and
helping the team overcome challenges.

A Scrum Master is a teacher, leader, and a change agent, capable
of building a team that can govern its own affairs and ultimately
making the team capable of operating without the scrum master's
intervention. However, not all scrum masters take delight in these
roles, instead considering their designation a way of moving up the
ladder. Then there are those who desire to be heroes via the role,
while others maintain the vision of becoming a scrum master,
perhaps inspired by another scrum master, for the inspirational
goodwill that the role may offer.

Situations abound where managers pick any available person to
become a scrum master. I have seen some people succeed in this

job and seen others grow weary and run out of the zeal it takes to continue. I have also seen some really thrive while others get exhausted, de-motivated, and eager to just run away.

There is more to becoming a good scrum master than zeal, focus, and motivation. Becoming a good scrum master goes beyond being determined, inspired, and excited to succeed. It requires soft skills and leadership plus a solid understanding of Agile, its principles, and practices. A good scrum master has the courage and will to learn despite challenges. The path can prove challenging, bumpy, and uneasy, but a good scrum master maintains courage and the will to learn. This book acts as a guide toward acquiring the necessary knowledge and the requisite skill set to succeed as scrum master.

I have been privileged to coach and train several scrum masters, executives, product owners, and teams in different countries and industries, so I offer here real-life experiences. In fact, most of the scenarios explained in this book are actual cases, but I have changed the names of individuals and organizations in order to protect anonymity.

My purpose is to provide information toward a good understanding of a scrum master's job, which is essential as many have indeed struggled with it. I intend to provide details about what the job entails so that others can more readily get traction toward success in the role. I hope my analysis of personal and life experiences will aid readers in better comprehending the role of scrum master, and I hope you might borrow, and learn, from my experience. Ultimately, this book acts as your guide for real-life situations.

I believe strongly that Agile is the best modern way of working. It empowers people, affords them authority, and pays attention to value, while at the same time creating a better workplace. My aim is that through this book's instructional processes, a reader may be prompted toward gaining the courage necessary to become a better scrum master, and in turn help readers realize their own dreams while motivating them to become better scrum masters.

Is this book for you?

THIS BOOK IS not a general introductory book; it contains contents specific to the subject of 'Agile Scrum Master' which means that the generic reader may not fully benefit from the book. If you are trying to become a Scrum Master or a Team Leader, however, you will benefit from book.

CHAPTER 1

Who is a Scrum Master?

W HO IS A scrum master, actually? That is one fundamental question anyone getting into Agile might ask. Before answering that question, though, let's consider what makes an Agile team.

Agile Team

An Agile team is an independent, self-organized team that provides value to the organization or its customers by making available a product or service. The team is made up of few team members, usually seven to nine, and it is always in contact with customers, other teams, and external parties like suppliers and service providers. In the process of fulfilling their role, the Agile team members decide how to organize their work and they choose the processes to follow. They live and breathe Agile values, principles, and practices. An Agile team consists of a scrum master, product owner, and development team, or simply the rest of the team members. The scrum master plays a major role in applying Agile values, principles, and practices.

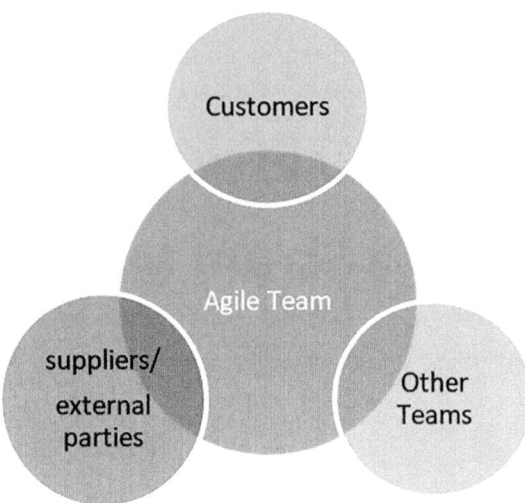

Figure 1: Interactions of an Agile Team

The Scrum Master

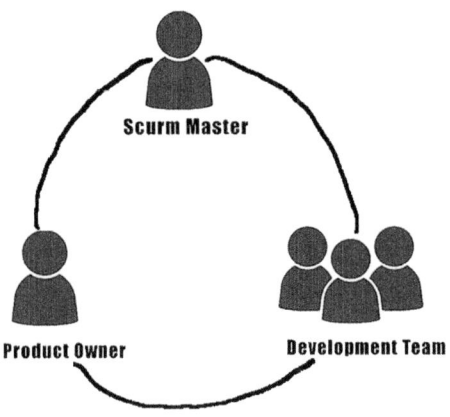

Figure 2: Agile Team

The scrum master has a significant role to play in building an independent, self-organized, and autonomous team. Since the scrum master understands the value of Agile principles and practices, he or she coaches and teaches the team on these very values. For that same reason, the scrum master helps the team adopt those principles and practices after teaching and coaching them on their value. He or she serves the team in many ways, which include facilitating team events, interactions, problem-solving events, team building, and removing impediments. The scrum master is the servant leader of the team.

With a knowledge of Agile values, principles, and practices, the scrum master ensures that customers and the organization understand this newest way of working. He or she becomes a change agent, advertising the Agile principle to the rest of the organization. The scrum master gets the team and the organization back on track if and when they fall into anti-Agile practices.

As already mentioned, the scrum master does much more than facilitating events, and this is the main reason this book is being made available. Scrum masters need to understand the responsibilities explained in the book and how to gain the required skills to thoroughly carry out these responsibilities.

A good scrum master is capable of building a good scrum team that delivers value to the customer and to the organization—and can convince any organization to adopt Agile principles and values as its new way of working. However, becoming a good scrum master is a journey that requires ample knowledge, technical skills, and passion.

CHAPTER 2

Scrum Master Maturity Model

I HAVE WATCHED SCRUM training many times, and in those trainings, a considerable amount of time (sometimes a few days) is allocated to discussing the scrum master's role. One common question posed during those trainings is, "**Who is qualified to be a scrum master?**"

Most trainers respond with, "Any team member can be a scrum master." Organizations who adhere to this statement appoint someone from the team as the scrum master and the results can be quite disastrous.

Naturally, I disagree with the notion that everyone and anyone is qualified for the role, and I urge all trainers to think twice about it. Not just any team member can be a scrum master because a scrum master must bring both leadership and facilitation skills to the table. Only a team member with those inherent skills can become a scrum master, and even then, only with proper coaching.

It is vital to understand the necessary maturity level of a scrum master, and also the level of support we as leaders and coaches have to give them so that they can move to the next level. The scrum master also needs to understand what skills to develop in order to gain the maturity required for the role. With this in mind, I propose the maturity model laid out in the table below.

I have considered many factors, such as Agile experience, leadership, and soft skills, when developing this simple maturity model.

Criterion	Maturity Level 0	Maturity Level 1	Maturity Level 2	Maturity Level 3
Has led a team before	No	No	Yes	Yes
Has been in an agile team before	No	No	Yes	Yes
Has been a Scrum Master before	No	No	Yes	Yes
Has experienced at least a scrum framework	No	No	Yes	Yes
Number of agile frameworks experienced	0	0	1 - 3	> 3
Number of agile teams led	0	0	1- 2	> 3
Agile certifications	No	No	Yes	Yes
Has leadership skills	No	Yes	Yes	Yes
Has some facilitation skill	No	Yes	Yes	Yes

This maturity level indicates who should be assigned the role of scrum master and what they should do to move to the next level.

Maturity Level 0:

In this level we assume that neither the scrum master nor the organization in which he or she works has experience in Agile. The organization may have decided to implement Agile and may have even selected a team; however, none of those personnel would know exactly how Agile works.

As the organization and the newly appointed team are new to Agile, both need to be carefully guided on the Agile journey. A well-experienced scrum master should be selected to lead such a team.

Criterion	Maturity Level 0
Has led a team before	No
Has been in an Agile Team before	No
Was a Scrum Master Before	No
Has experienced at least a Scrum Framework	No
Number of Agile frameworks experienced	0
Number of Agile teams led	0
Agile certifications	No
Has leadership skills?	No
Has facilitations kills?	No

Case Study

Planet Oil (a fictitious name) is a global oil and gas company which operates in almost every country. As part of the new way of working, the organization started implementing Agile as a pilot project. One European country joined the pilot project, and all the teams in one business division that were part of the pilot project were given scrum training.

Neil, one of the attendees of the training, was enthusiastic about becoming a scrum master after attending two days of scrum training. Managers supported the decision to give him the role, admitting that they had no clue who would make the best scrum master and because most of the other team members were reluctant to volunteer for something that was a complete change from how they had been working.

There was a coach assigned to the team and, under the guidance of the coach, Neil learned his responsibilities. Just in the middle of the second sprint, however, the Agile coach realized Neil was not the right choice for the role of scrum master after all. Neil himself realized it as well: he was under stress and could not meet the team's expectations. For example, the team would say, "Scrum master, can you schedule a meeting to get the review done?" By day's end, Neil had accumulated too many requests from the team about booking this meeting or that meeting. He could not ask the team, "What stopped you from booking the meeting yourselves?" or, "Let me help you book the meeting this time but next time you do it yourselves."

In another instance related to time boxing, Neil would start the stopwatch on his phone but never ended the discussion when the timer went off. Moreover, he was apprehensive to tell the managers who the team members were that caused the time run out. Neil simply lacked leadership skills. He was becoming an administrator to the team instead of its 'servant leader.'

Leadership skills are something that take time to develop. In essence, such candidates should be given the opportunity to realize what it takes to be a scrum master and thereafter be given an opportunity to be one if they so desire.

The point here is that if you happen to be this person who was so enthusiastic about Agile but had never really worked on such projects before, or had not ever even seen any Agile projects, just slow down and seek guidance, mentoring, and coaching from a good Agile coach before you truly take on the scrum master role.

Maturity Level 1

At this level, you have not really experienced any Agile projects or been a scrum master for an Agile project, but you clearly have good leadership and facilitation skills. In this case, you can be a scrum master if you so desire, but only under the supervision of a capable Agile coach who can guide you seamlessly throughout the project.

At the beginning, the Agile coach can run the first few sprints, with you as scrum master shadowing and facilitating small sessions such as stand-ups. Later on, the coach can guide you in facilitating other sessions, such as sprint planning and sprint reviews. After five or six sprints, you should be ready to take care of all scrum ceremonies.

Coaching is important as you will likely develop many questions and not know exactly what to do or what behaviors to showcase as a scrum master. Also, it is possible that you may fall back into the 'command and control' style of directing the team when things become tough. For example, a scrum master I knew started controlling the team members' calendar schedule, saying, "Things should be time-boxed." Misrepresentations or misunderstandings of Agile principles and practices can happen, so some one-on-one personal Agile coaching is essential at this level.

Another factor to consider is the amount of time such scrum masters need to spend. There are many things to learn and some are time consuming, hence it is important that such candidates are committed, full-time, to the scrum master's role.

Criterion	Maturity Level 1
Has led a team before	No
Has been in an Agile Team before	No
Has been a scrum master before	No
Has experienced at least a scrum framework	No
Number of agile frameworks experienced	0
Number of agile teams led	0
Agile certifications	No
Has leadership skills	Yes
Has facilitation skills	Yes

As an example, if you are a new scrum master who has never before really led any scrum teams, or if you have not been part of any scrum teams but have good leadership skills, you can take up a scrum master's role, but you should not take up responsibility for two scrum teams simultaneously. It is a classic recipe for failure. Leaders also have a responsibility here and should avoid assigning multiple Agile projects to new scrum masters as that can burn them out, and the benefits expected out of them may not be reaped.

Maturity Level 2:

At this level, you have some good experience as a scrum master. You at least have experience with the scrum framework and have led at least one Agile team successfully. What this says is that you know scrum ceremonies, which include sprint planning, stand-ups, backlog refinement, sprint reviews, and retrospectives, and the

Agile way of working such as self-organization, time boxing, servant leadership, and relative estimations. For example, you can explain relative estimation to the team and even challenge a project manager who is asking to implement a number of hours as estimation.

However, there remains so much to learn. For example, consider how you would react if the team constantly said, "Retrospectives are useless and a waste of time." Would you listen to the team and give up retrospectives? Thorough knowledge on at least one Agile framework makes you a thought leader and helps the team to be more agile. However, you should try to expand your knowledge beyond the framework you know.

It is vital to begin studying or learning other Agile frameworks like Kanban, Large Scale Scrum, and Spotify. You can also seek out mentorship from an Agile coach. This experience would give you a better shot at supporting two or three scrum teams concurrently, as you would know better how to self-organize.

Criterion	Maturity Level 2
Has led a team before	Yes
Has been in an agile team before	Yes
Has been a scrum master before	Yes
Has experienced at least a scrum framework	Yes
Number of agile frameworks experienced	1
Number of agile teams led	1 to 2
Agile certifications	Yes
Has leadership skills	Yes
Has facilitation skills	Yes

Maturity Level 3:

You are at this level if you have successfully led many Agile teams and have experienced other Agile frameworks. This simply means you can recommend suitable Agile frameworks depending on the project and can probably start mentoring scrum master candidates of maturity level 0 or 1.

You can also work independently without much support from a senior Agile coach. You contribute actively to the Agile community of practice, write a few blogs, or even share your experience at Agile talks.

Criterion	Maturity Level 3
Has led a team before	Yes
Has been in an agile team before	Yes
Was a scrum master before	Yes
Has experienced at least a scrum framework	Yes
Number of agile frameworks experienced	more than 3
Number of agile teams led	more than 3
Agile certifications	Yes
Has leadership skills	Yes
Has facilitation skills	Yes

At this level, you must have applied to coach or have coached your own teams and have been identified as a real master in the frameworks you have been practicing. You must be passionate about what you are doing and have the knowledge to solve big problems.

You must know the limitations of the current framework, so that solutions come naturally to you.

However, you should never stop studying large Agile frameworks like SAFe. You should recognize the benefits of Agile frameworks to organizations and start to teach them.

Summary

Becoming a scrum master is sometimes a dream for some people, while for others it happens by chance. You may consciously select it as your career, but that decision should be made carefully as it comes with a necessary commitment and investment. While some of your natural strengths can prove helpful, there are other skills one must learn in the quest. The maturity model I have proposed can be a useful aid; use it to assess where you fit in the maturity model, and then follow the necessary steps to move to the next levels with proper guidance and coaching.

CHAPTER 3

Scrum Master's success Recipe

OST OF THE time when I conduct Agile trainings, I am asked, "What does it take to become a good, successful scrum master?" My answer is typically simple and straightforward:

"Agile knowledge, facilitations skill, and leadership."

Most Agile trainers would say, "Anyone in the team can be a scrum master," which is true up to a certain level. Anyone on the team "can be a scrum master," but that does not guarantee he or she becomes a successful scrum master. As an explanation, I offer below an example.

Case Study

James is a content editor by profession. The marketing division in which he has been working has been selected to host the first Agile project in the organization. It has been going through an Agile transformation and has decided to take baby steps by starting a pilot project. As a result, his entire business division has been sent for a two-day scrum training featuring theoretical and hands-on exercises.

Full scrum simulation was enacted over two days of training. James volunteered to be the scrum master during these simulations.

When his project was selected for the scrum pilot, then, management selected James as the scrum master. One reason James was chosen was his friendliness to others on the team. He had good rapport with everyone, and he did not oppose the idea.

The Agile coach explained to James what the responsibilities of a scrum master are, the events he had to facilitate, and how to facilitate them. He also had a daily one-on-one coaching session with James.

During week one, the Agile coach facilitated the ceremonies while James shadowed him. The objective was to have James facilitate the scrum ceremonies from week two onwards. In the second week, then, it was James' turn to facilitate and organize team activities, but James had not yet picked up the skills.

As an example, during review sessions with external parties, James carried out facilitation with time boxing but never adhered to time. He would set a 15-minutes alarm for one topic but would end up resetting the time and taking his seat to listen to the topic as the team continued the discussion. By the end of the two-hour time box, the objectives of the meeting were not met. The team blamed James for not alerting them when they exceeded the scheduled time box.

In another instance, John, a team member, informed James that Nick, a marketing manager who was supposed to give approval to John, had failed to do so over and over; as a result, John was unable to complete his work. He reiterated this position a few times during standup, but James just told John he should somehow seek and effectively get the approval he needed from Nick.

The Agile coach urged James to reach out to Nick and try to set an appointment. He agreed to do so but never followed through. The Agile coach realized that Jame's hesitancy to reach out to Nick was due to the inherent hierarchy: in other words, Nick held a higher rank than James and that made James tentative to reach out.

James was a follower, not a servant leader. Within a few weeks he had a pile of tasks yet to be completed, and the team lost the confidence in him. This was compounded by the fact that sprint goals were repeatedly missed.

During coaching sessions, the Agile coach would make some suggestions and James would agree with them, but eventually he would end up not acting on them. James then started skipping coaching sessions, and finally he was too stressed out and he expressed his wish to move to a different team.

The successful scrum masters I have encountered embark on a continuous learning journey that makes them good scrum masters. They prefer this style of working as it allows them to gain more Agile knowledge. The following chapters will explain the knowledge scrum masters need to acquire in order to become good at their work.

Agile Knowledge

It is essential scrum masters have a good, in-depth knowledge of Agile.

According to Agile Alliance, the scrum master is, "the person who ensures that the team adheres to agile values and principles and follows the processes and practices that the team agreed to follow". Almost all Agile professionals expect a scrum master to live up to Agile values and principles and help the team cultivate them. This is not possible if the scrum master does not have good knowledge of Agile.

Scrum master is the change agent

A scrum master plays a major role as the agent of change, helping to cultivate Agile values and practices within the team. In addition, product owners who may come from traditional, functional backgrounds also look up to the scrum master to understand the Agile practices; thus, a scrum master must have a solid knowledge of Agile.

The Agile knowledge that any scrum master must possess is clarified below:

- Knowledge on Agile manifestoes and Agile values
- Knowledge on Agile principles
- Knowledge on different Agile frameworks

The chapters to come will explain these three areas in detail.

CHAPTER 4

Knowledge on agile manifesto and agile values

THERE IS NO one in the Agile community who has not heard about the Agile manifesto, since almost all Agile training sessions begin with the manifesto as a starting point. As the change agent of Agile, the scrum master needs to know the real meaning behind Agile manifesto.

Individuals and interactions over processes and tools

Working software over comprehensive documentation

Customer collaboration over contract negotiation

Responding to change over following a plan

These are the fundamental building blocks on which Agile is built. A scrum master must be able to adequately explain these principles to the team, rather than simply reiterating the bullet points like a parrot. Below is an explanation of the Agile manifesto.

Individuals and interactions over processes and tools

Processes have a significant place in the corporate world. We have heard the phrase, "It is the process," "We have to follow due process," "That is how things are done here," "Cannot bypass the process, and "Processes are there for a reason."

Processes are created to make things better, but when these processes are blindly followed, they can make things go more slowly than necessary. As a result, value delivery to the customer is delayed. The funny part is that most of the time, people do not know why such processes exist. In such situations, processes become a burden rather than an aid. This brings to life the first item in the manifesto.

Why Individuals and Interactions?

Unnecessary processes add delay. They do not talk to humans hence they really do not care about the outcome. That is why we sometimes have to put a face to them. For example, having a meeting via voice-over is different from a face-to-face meeting. While the former can be a bit harsh, the latter is more humane.

I recall Sunny. Sunny was team leader of an external team with which my team worked. The completion of my team's work depended on input Sunny was supposed to provide; however, week after week the work was delayed due to a lack of input from him. He declined each meeting my team scheduled and gave no positive feedback to the daily correspondence my team sent. One fine day, Sunny sent a message to my team saying he was following due process, but he was lacking necessary input from my as a priority. In the meantime, my team was thinking differently, as among the output items we were producing was one report very critical to decision making. Hence, my team was under pressure while Sunny was not.

As a last resort, I paid Sunny a visit. Based on email communication, my perception of Sunny was that he was a lousy, rough around the edges, unpolished professional, but my visit proved me wrong.

I saw a slight, innocent-looking young man behind the big monitor. His body language showed that things were not going well. I introduced myself to him and he came across as polite. In other words, my perception couldn't have been more off the mark. We chatted for a few minutes about the day (not about work), then he revealed some information of which I was unaware.

His boss had resigned, and all of his workload had been transferred to Sunny. Also, one of Sunny's team members was on maternity leave, which simply meant he had three people's workload to do and he also had to leave for India in one week's time for his brother's wedding. He was under real pressure. The reason for his body language soon dawned on me. He felt badly that he had not been able to spare any time for us, but what happened next surprised me. He scheduled an hour's meeting with my team to have a quick review of the report, and he promised more time once he returned from his trip. That was exactly what we had wanted. I am quite certain that sending mails and meeting reports would never have gotten his attention and this valuable input.

We are dealing with people NOT machines.

This is something we should always remember, along with the notion that these people have hearts and souls. We must treat them as human beings. When we put people first, they can do anything for us. That is why Richard Branson says, "**Take care of people and they will take care of business.**"

When we put people at the core and heart of the business, then the whole dynamic changes. There is nothing in the world that cannot be solved by discussion, negotiations, and face-to-face interactions.

Working software over comprehensive documentation

Sarah joined a not-for-profit organization as a project manager. The project she was to manage had started ten months before, but the project manager and the business analysts leading the project had resigned earlier, which is how Sarah came to be put in charge.

An external consultancy company had developed a solution which was to go live by December, i.e., within two months' time, according to the plan. When Sarah joined, the PMO Manager handed her three big folders. The first contained the contract and the project plan, the second was the requirements documents, and the third was the solutions design and the detailed documents. Each was over two hundred pages long, apart from the contract. She determined that they were all up-to-date documents, as the last update had been done just five days prior by the previous project manager. She tried to read it within a short time but could not get a good picture, and so she asked the product owner to give her access to the test environment so that she could have a look at the software which was supposed to go live in two months.

"What test environment? We don't have a test environment" came the response from the product owner, obviously surprised by Sarah's request.

"According to this contract," Sarah pointed to a page within the contract, "you guys should have by now been provided with a test environment," Sarah explained.

"No, we haven't actually," the product owner explained.

Then Sarah called Ashley, the counterpart project manager of the consultancy company, who acknowledged there had been some miscommunication. They were supposed to release the test environment but somehow missed getting it rolled out. She assured Sarah that the test environment would be released within a couple of days, but this turned out to be just the beginning of the contradictions between reality and what was represented in the document. Sarah also found out that the solution was not yet ready to be released, even though the project status reports indicated it was ready and in green. That means according to the project status report, everything was going smooth. But in the reality, it was not.

The above is a real case. There was a nice set of documents but no working solution to be used by customers, even after ten months. All the money and effort had been spent on creating a pile of documentation instead of making the product work.

This is a common pattern in software development (and common as well in other functions, such as human resources, marketing, and finance), especially where the solution is outsourced. Teams are encouraged to create ample documentation and status reports as proof of the solution.

Awareness of this problem should cause us to think differently. If an organization has a problem, then a working solution, not a bunch of documents, is required – and soon. That is why Agile prioritizes developing and delivering a working solution over creating a slew of documents, which do nothing toward solving a problem.

However, there are sometimes genuine reasons to justify documentation, although they cannot be anything like what is explained next.

"I need documentation because I am not clear on the requirements." Such a demand hints at the details of the requirements, so the solution should be to seek clarity, not documentation. And how can one get clarity? Probably by asking more detail-oriented questions, then discuss the requirements, brainstorm about them, and rephrase your understanding of them. Develop a prototype to validate the requirements, and that will make it possible to clarify the requirements.

Genuine reasons for having documentation might include legislation or regulations; beyond those, I believe that documentation is a lightweight process and should be reduced to the bare minimum. If time is spent on building a working solution, and on getting continuous feedback, that solution would come more readily.

Customer collaboration over contract negotiation

What is a contract?

The *Oxford Dictionary* defines a 'contract' as a "written or spoken agreement, especially one concerning employment, sales, or tenancy, which is intended to be enforceable by law." Commercial contracts come to mind where a customer and a service provider are involved, and where an exchange of product or service is required.

Service providers offer certain services or products to the customer and in return customers offer to pay the price of the service or product. In this situation, contracts are made a major part of this transactional process.

Complications

Service providers tend to write down what services they have agreed to offer and at what price. Customers tend to write down what they are expected to receive and at what price. The issue with this process is the amount of detail a contract requires. Some organizations hire commercial lawyers who specialize in the respective field. The contract writing process can run the time span of several months, and as a result, customers do not get the anticipated value in time. Instead of fixing the problem when there is a problem with a delivered product, we check the terms of contract to see if any agreement was breached. If the agreement has not been breached, we then check how much should be charged to the customer for us to correct the problem. This adds more burden to the customer, who ends up suffering by not having the correct product or service. That is where contracts are becoming a burden.

Negotiate instead

It is best to check what needs to be done to fix the issue instead of going back and forth. It is best to understand the problem, discuss with the customer, and then negotiate for a solution. In my experience, customers tend to be flexible in terms of cost and in dealing with the delay necessary to solve an issue, at least when the service provider is authentic. Thus, putting more effort into building a relationship with the customer is required, as is effort at negotiating with the customer, instead of engaging in lengthy, unproductive, and wasteful contract creation processes.

Responding to change over following a plan

Why change?

According to Buddha, the only permanent thing is 'change.' Although this philosophy is grounded in spirituality, there is a valuable truth in it transferrable to other spheres. When we consider our working environments, what we see is constant change. In my short working history of twenty years, I have seen how computers are taking over the manual work processes and also how the internet is taking over connections, relationships, and communications. Even just since the nineties, I have noticed how mobile phones have invaded most of our lives and other small devices like wearables have literally taken over. Change is everywhere and there is no way of stopping it. I experienced the wave of change in a specific work environment when I worked for a global company for around four years. There I witnessed three customer relationship management systems, namely Siebel, SAP CRM, and Salesforce CRM. Those systems were introduced because the existing systems could not cater to emerging demands, so in short, the company introduced a new system that could meet higher mandates.

Speed of change and digital disruption.

The speed at which change happens is phenomenal. Customers change their minds all the time, and to be frank, they do not do so because they want to. Rather, they are forced to, and as a result, new systems to cater to those requirements are required. Changing something which has already been built is not easy, but we should understand that it is better to make partners with the customers rather than to complain about them and the changes they demand.

For example, it would be sad, and also time and money consuming, to build a mobile phone based on a customer's requirement only for the customer to change his or her mind.

This is why it is better to make the changes earlier and to also engage the customer—the very one who will use the solution we are seeking—during the change process. Essentially, we need to take a collaborative approach with the customer.

In my previous example of the 'not-for-profit company,' the consulting company did not engage the customer early enough, but they created a wonderful project plan and sent weekly updates to the client. Since they did not engage the client in the development stage, the changes the client later requested proved difficult to implement. That damages the relationship between the two parties.

Need details on Agile manifesto?

What we are trying to do in this chapter is to get some understanding of the Agile manifesto, which explains the issues we encounter in the development process, and how the process can be made better. But in any case, the reader can find more detail about the Agile manifesto by seeking out some of the existing literature about it.

There are in fact many books on the Agile manifesto, and below are a few suggestions.

Author: Jamie Lynn Cooke

Name: *Agile Principles Unleashed*

Amazon link : https://www.amazon. com.au/Agile-Principles-Unleashed-Jamie-Cooke/dp/1849280576/ref=sr_1 _13?ie=UTF8&qid=1528505001&sr=8-13&keywords=agile+principles

Author: Larry Apke

Name: Understanding The Agile Manifesto: A Brief & *Bold Guide to Agile*

But if the argument is why one would buy *another* book when the current book is already in hand, rest assured that the basics of Agile will indeed be covered for you.

CHAPTER 5

Agile Principals

THIS CHAPTER IS aimed at developing a reader's knowledge of the Agile principles.

As the scrum master, you are the advocate, for the team and the organization, of Agile principles. You are therefore expected to have an excellent knowledge of Agile principles, and these are built upon the Agile manifesto. To come is a more in-depth analysis of Agile principles and their meaning. First, a list of Agile principles as per the scrum framework.

1. The highest priority is to satisfy the customer through early and continuous delivery of valuable software.

2. Welcome changing requirements even when it is late in the product development. Agile processes harness change for the customer's competitive advantage.

3. Deliver working software frequently, from a couple of weeks to a couple of months, with preference to the shorter timescale.

4. Business people and developers must work together daily throughout the project.

5. Build projects around motivated individuals, giving them the environment and support they need and also trusting them to get the job done.

6. The most efficient and effective method of conveying information to and within a development team is face-to-face conversation.

7. Working software is the primary measure of progress.

8. Agile processes promote sustainable development. The sponsors, developers, and users should be able to maintain indefinitely a constant pace.

9. Continuous attention to technical excellence and good design enhance agility.

10. Simplicity, the art of maximizing the amount of work not done, is essential.

11. The best architecture, requirements, and designs emerge from self-organizing teams.

12. At regular intervals, the team reflects on how to become more effective, then tunes and adjusts its behavior accordingly.

In-depth analysis of Agile principles

In the following section, these agile principles will be explained in detail.

1. The highest priority is to satisfy the customer through early and continuous delivery of valuable software.

For any business to succeed, it needs to keep delivering value to its customers. And when we talk about value delivery, this value needs to be delivered when it is required and not after months of delay.

Why it is important to deliver value early?

Imagine you are in a restaurant and very hungry. If the chef is taking about one hour to prepare your meal, you will likely be dissatisfied because you would like to begin eating.

But in a situation where meal preparation time lingers, and a customer could be offered an appetizer while he waits, that customer would at least be happy to have something to nibble in the moment. By the time the appetizer is finished, the main meal would likely be ready. The time it takes from when one places an order to when the meal is delivered is important to any customer.

If a restaurant has a long serve time, the customer might stop visiting that restaurant, even though it might serve the best food around.

Big Bang versus incremental delivery

In my previous example of 'Service Now,' late product delivery in not-for-benefit organizations leads to such chaos, and it is created by many factors. One main reason is that delivery is scheduled to be done at one go. This is most common in many product deliveries. However, this should not be the case.

This is where incremental delivery comes into the picture. There is no point waiting for a year or longer to receive a product; instead, the most important product features can be prioritized and delivered first. Then, lesser priority product features can be delivered later or not delivered at all. Since some of those features are really low priority features, customers would not be upset, even if they were not delivered. Sometimes, it can be economical to avoid delivery of the least prioritized items.

2. Welcome changing requirements, even late in development

The last time I visited a bookstore was about six months ago in Singapore. I loved my visits to Kinokunia since it has a huge collection of books. It also has nice ambience and a library where anyone can comfortably sit and read through books.

It even has a café where one can have a coffee while skimming through books to decide about buying, or just sit and chat with a friend about a book which has just been released. In contrast, I visit the Amazon online bookstore almost every day.

Normally, I buy more books on Amazon than in a normal bookstore. What this simply says is that our consumer patterns have changed drastically. It means businesses that used to have us as customers, face real challenges due to these consumer behavior changes. Businesses are forced to constantly fight back and figure out how to adapt to these changes. So, if you were in the business of software or service provision, then your customer would require you to adapt to these changes as well.

In traditional software development, however, changes are not welcome, and I attribute that to the waterfall delivery model where the requirements are first captured, signed off on by the customer, then moved into the development phase. Also, I believe that the architecture of the software has been designed as fixed, so any changes done later are bound to be costly to implement.

Welcoming changes

The traditional strategy, or way of development, does not favor the customer nor does it welcome changes. However, since changes are inevitable, we need to facilitate the ones customers request by changing our development process in order to accommodate those changes.

3. Deliver working software frequently, from a couple of weeks to a couple of months, with a preference to the shorter timescale.

This principle goes hand in hand with the second principle of welcoming changes even in the late stages of the development cycle.

Even though this principle is about software, it is applicable in business aspects. Agile principles are now being applied in business operations. For example, auditing, HR, marketing, and sales are done by applying Agile principles.

One of the main reasons traditional waterfall development fails is that the working software is delivered as a big bang, sometimes once in several months or once a year. Take the example of the 'Service Now' application discussed earlier. It was released to the customer after twelve months, but that application has several modules like incident, problem management, change and release management, and configurations management, all of which could have been easily released earlier in the production life cycle rather than releasing everything after twelve months.

This principle is closely related to the psychological side of change management. Suppose a man is addicted to smoking and due to health issues, his doctor has advised him to quit, essentially to stay alive. A chain smoker would find it difficult to heed that advice, since as an addict, he would not know how. Smoking for such a person is like breathing. He simply cannot stop.

But what if he breaks this big change down into smaller chunks and tries to achieve the smaller chunk first. For instance, if you were a smoker and you tried to cut down on smoking, the body would react to the new change. It would be difficult to handle such depravation, which is why some people experience shivering and breathing problems when they try to reduce their smoking.

What if you tried the slow and steady approach? Suppose you consume thirty cigarettes a day, but you reduce that number by one cigarette each day, or if that is difficult, then by smoking one fewer per week. This small step does the trick. First, psychologically this step is approachable, friendly, and digestible. If we asked a smoker, "Can you stop smoking your thirty cigarettes a day?" he would go nuts. But if we posed the question, "Can you reduce your smoking by one cigarette a day?" he would be more open and reply, "Yeah, I can try."

Without the acceptance from the person going through the change, success of the entire change introduction would be unlikely. Chances are, if you were to miss out one cigarette a day out of thirty, your body would not even recognize the difference, hence a feeling of achievement would result. Consequently, you might be motivated to reduce your smoking by one more cigarette on the second day. That means by the end of thirty days, with little effort, you could have completely changed and would no longer need any cigarettes.

This also applies to those consuming the solutions built by IT teams. If you introduce a change in big bang, there is a probability the change would be resisted, and these people would see you as the problem maker. Also, if the customer does not like it, a slew of negative feedback will come all at once, and that can overwhelm you and your team. It may also cost money to accommodate the design changes all at once, which is why software development teams are not that motivated after a product release, and frankly, they often feel terrible.

As such, we should try and reduce this change impact by adding value to the customer, which is ultimately the goal of any service provider.

How do we apply this Agile principle?

That is where iterative developments come into the picture. We should aim at delivering working software at the end of every sprint/ iteration. Here an iteration can be two weeks, three weeks, or even four weeks. If we cannot achieve that, then in my opinion we have not added any value to the customer.

A typical example is one of my latest products, where our team was responsible for developing reporting dashboards to indicate the latest infrastructure roll out in the country. Our team, whose members were not used to the concept of early releases, sometimes took more than a month to release the report to the business, which continued to roll out the network on the ground on a daily basis. When the business is moving this quickly and those involved are being informed of the status on a monthly basis, it does not add any value to the business as work will already have been completed by the time they receive the report. In other words, such a report would be old data. Finally, this team managed to release major reporting dashboards once every two weeks, which the customer appreciated.

As a scrum master, you should be able to explain this to the team and get them to fully understand it, then make the changes necessary to enable regular release of the product to the customer.

There are multiple advantages associated with regular release of the product.

Why quick feedback is important

When the release is small in terms of changes, the effort required to release it for production is relatively small. Hence, the production or operations team responsible for making the necessary changes within the production system is able to incorporate the software changes that have been developed without much of a hassle.

However, when it is a big change being requested after three months or a year, the production team, configuration management teams, and even the operations teams must do a variety of activities, and this does not go well for the relationship between the operation and development teams. This is the same reason some development and operations teams work weekends and also round the clock when big releases about to be made.

Conversely, customers who use the system or the product may encounter problems, and if feedback is received soon, such problems can be quickly rectified and the product released back to the customer. If, however, feedback is not sent within a short time, then the issues pile up, and then considerably more time and effort are required to rectify things and then to release a suitable solution.

4. Businesspeople and developers must work together daily throughout the project

Everyone has had the experience of calling a bakery or a pastry shop and ordering the cake we want, explaining the details regarding flavor, occasion, colors, and size. We do all of that over the phone, then the baker asks whether we want a message written on the cake. One such caller instructed the baker as below:

"Please write 'Best Wishes, Suzanne,' and underneath that write, 'We will miss you'."

The caller came to the shop the next day to pick up the cake and was shocked to see below (Figure 3):

Figure 3: Misinterpreted requirements (Cackerecks.com)

In this instance, no doubt the pastry chef was skillful, but the message completely missed the point and as such, the cake was useless. If the customer did not go crazy, he or she must have been a saint.

Cake Wrecks is a web site that has a huge repository of cake decorations gone wrong. Check it out at http://cakewrecks.com.

This happens all the time in product development, whether it is in software or any other product development.

Both parties suffer

I have been at both ends of the spectrum, one as a customer and the other as the supplier. As a customer, one becomes frustrated and disappointed and considers it a waste of money and time because to not receive the correct product at the right time. On the other hand, the development team spends plenty of time and effort making the product and when the customer rejects it, the team is really disappointed, taking it as a personal failure.

These are two sides to the same coin, and communication gaps are the root cause of the problem.

Figure 4: Collaboration between customer and development team

Mediators

When the customer is separated from the development team, like in traditional software development, the interaction between two teams is minimal and formal because the interactions happen via meetings, workshops, and status update sessions. Limited formal communications often go wrong. The development team may not understand the details of the customer's problem or the requirements in general.

Value delivery.

Our main focus is value delivery. In this process, then, we should remove any processes that contribute to delays. The development team's separation from the customer reduces communication, which adds delays in the value delivery process.

Instead of treating customers as outsiders to the development teams, we should make them part of the development teams. Co-creating the product with the customer reduces communication gaps and adds some additional benefits as follows:

- This builds shared ownership of the problem and the solution.

- The builds a better relationship between the two teams.

- This provides the opportunity for instant feedback on the developed product, minimizing waste.

- This leads to many more future engagements as customers as well as the development company understand each other's strengths.

- This leaves minimal room for cost increases that normally come from change requests or reworks, thanks to a minimization of waste.

- This leads to co-creation, which is good for development companies since they can finish the work as fast as possible and get their resources freed to be utilized in a different project.

5. Build projects around motivated individuals. Give them the environment and support they need and trust them to get the job done.

I have in the past played the role of project manager. I should say I was pretty new on the job though I knew how to come up with a project plan. Before that appointment, I had only once been an IT business analyst and my job had been to bridge the IT side and the business side of the solution (notably, this was pre-Agile).

I consulted my team, and each person had estimations regarding the duration the work would take. After consolidating the work plan, the project duration came up being thirteen months. I then added a contingency based on the uncertainty we had, and the final project plan expanded to seventeen months. I reviewed the plan with the team, and we were all confident about the estimated time we had agreed upon.

I went to the Program Manager and presented the plan and he declared that our estimate must have been incorrect because a solution like that ordinarily took only six months. "You must be kidding," I thought to myself. As a software engineer and a business analyst, I knew for sure that that type of a complex solution could not be done within six months. But as a junior manager, I did not have the confidence to challenge and negotiate. Instead, I came back to the team and explained the Program Manager's expectation. They went nuts.

Finally, with difficulty, we settled on twelve months, which the Program Manager promptly changed to six months after reducing the contingencies on the basis that we were prone to complicating things. "Why did you ask that a project plan be created if you knew it was going to take six months?" I thought to myself.

Anyhow, the plan was sold to the senior managers and the project kicked off.

However, we finished the project after thirteen months, not six.

KNOWLEDGE WORKERS CAN DO WONDERS

Peter Ducker uses the term 'knowledge workers' to refer to the people we call workers. He argues that 'workers' know the 'work' better than managers, hence they are 'knowledge workers. Managers do not need to tell knowledge workers how to do the job; managers simply need to trust knowledge workers and build an environment where the team can perform at their best.

SCRUM MASTER'S ROLE

Scrum masters play a key role in building a self-organized team. When you build the right environment and give autonomy to the knowledge workers, they will do the job. This is discussed in detail in the coming chapters.

6. The most efficient and effective method of conveying information to and within a development team is face-to-face conversation.

RESEARCH SAYS

In 2008, Forbes conducted a survey by asking 750 business executives whether they liked to travel for business meetings to conduct those meetings face-to-face, or if they preferred to save money and conduct the meetings using technology- enabled remote services. Fifty-eight percent of respondents replied that they liked to travel to conduct face-to-face meetings, irrespective of travel costs (Forbes Insights, 2009).

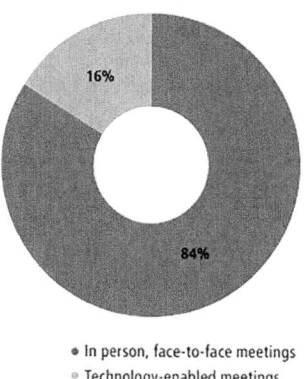

• In person, face-to-face meetings
⦿ Technology-enabled meetings

Figure 5: Face to Face meeting vs Technology enabled meetings
(Forbes Insights,2009)

When asked why, they provided a series of answers as explained below.

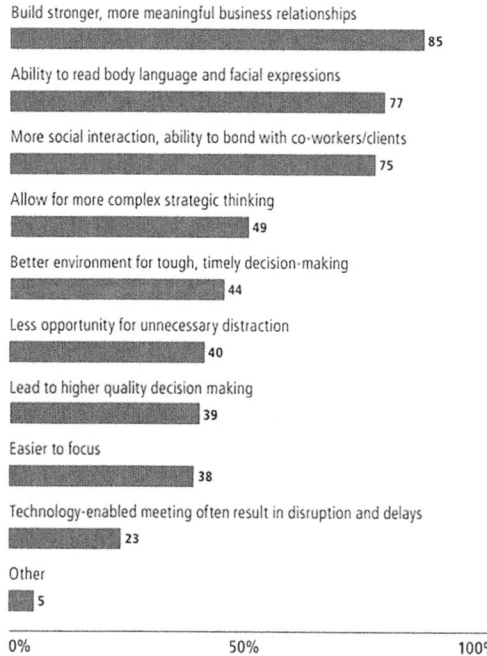

Figure 6: Executive view on why Face to Face meetings are better
(Forbes Insights,2009)

One of the research studies I conducted revealed the same results. If we link team performance to face-to-face communications, we see there is a strong correlation and better outcomes compared to the situations without face-to-face communications.

SPEED Matters.

We are in a stage where speed is important and where decisions are made quickly in order to respond to changes that continuously crop up. Information is required to make appropriate decisions, and the faster such information is made available, the faster the decisions can be made.

We have many communication mediums to convey information, email, telephone, and electronic messaging systems like chats to name a few. Another communication medium is face-to-face communication, which is unique as it makes possible the transference of more than just the information.

WHY FACE-TO-FACE COMMUNICATION IS THE BEST

In other words, there is another dimension to the information from face-to-face communication beyond what one gets from other communication mediums. For example, if you meet a team member and talk to the person about an issue found in the code, apart from the technical information you derive from the talk, you also get to learn more hidden information through the person's body language. You learn how hard the person has tried to resolve the problem, for example, but you would not have gotten this vital information if the communication happened via electronic means.

If the person seems too tired, you can probably figure out that he has exhausted all the possibilities of developing a solution, and you may need to either get help from another or give this person more time. Decision making in a face-to-face communication is quicker and more negotiation can be done.

In Agile, our focus is on building autonomous, self-organized teams. Team winning is much more important than individual winning when we focus on delivering value to the customer. That means that any obstacles or delays in the value stream need to be resolved quickly, and face-to-face communication plays a key role in doing so.

7. Working software is the primary measure of progress.

PROGRESS REPORTS.

In every project we create progress reports, which indicate the progress of planned work against the actual work. For example, if the plan says Product Increment 1 should be ready by the end of June, we ought to check by June to see the progress. These progress reports play a key role in the progression of product development, and as such all teams make extra effort to generate them at regular intervals. Depending on the urgency of the product, reports are generated on a daily, weekly, or monthly basis.

WATERMELON REPORTS

However, what is communicated in the report and the reality of the actual product can be very different: we call these reports 'watermelon reports.' It is green (indicating good) on the outside, but once you cut it open, it is all red (indicating not so good).

This was the case in my previous example of the 'SERVICE NOW' project. The reports produced by the consultancy company indicated all green, meaning in progress with no issues, but after spending nine months on the project, the solution was not workable. Nobody could use the product at all, not even a test version of it.

If the product is not in a consumable position, then all the effort was futile, because to deliver value the product needs to be consumable.

WORKING SOFTWARE SHOULD BE THE PRIMARY FOCUS.

Consequently, our focus should be on making a consumable, working software instead of making a bunch of non-consumable reports. We have multiple Agile practices that have been developed using this principle, one good example being the creation of visual performance indicators like the Kanban walls. The Kanban wall emits information on the progress of the reports, which means there is no need for special reports.

Creation of products in increments is also based on this principle. The entire product may not be produced within a short time span, but product increments are released at regular intervals, ideally at the end of every sprint.

8. Agile processes promote sustainable development. The sponsors, developers, and users should be able to maintain indefinitely a constant pace.

Agile is all about self-organized teams delivering value to the customer by maintaining optimal speed and pace for a longer period. That means the team needs to decide how they are going to operate and at what speed. Unlike other methods of product or service development, Agile is a pull system.

PUSH SYSTEMS vs PULL SYSTEM

Most of the traditional product/project teams operate as push systems. That means the managers push work to the team and the team do that work. This works in the short-term and attracts overtime for the team, who end up working for long hours and weekends only to become tired and demotivated, thereby producing poor quality products. Agile is trying to avoid such a situation.

Instead of pushing work, Agile tries to maintain sustainability by creating a pull system. What does this mean? Agile has created a few practices for building a pull system, and these include the team deciding the capacity or load it can take up on a regular basis. This is normally known as 'velocity.' In the pull system, the team pulls work based on the priorities set by the customer or product owner. This way, the customer gets the anticipated value, yet the team does not experience burn out.

9. Continuous attention to technical excellence and good design enhances agility.

Simple can be harder than complex; you have to work hard to get your thinking clean to make it simple.—Steve Jobs

I once visited one of my friends in Bangalore, India, where his family lived in a high-rise apartment complex. His apartment was on the sixth floor. Since it was an old building, they did not have an elevator, just stairs. Every time they wanted something outside, they had to walk down and then walk back up again. That means they had to plan better about when to go down and for what. Meanwhile, they had found a clever way of transporting some items like fish, vegetables, and the like from the ground floor to the sixth floor.

Simple system that serve the purpose

In India, it is common for fish mongers and vegetable sellers to go from door to door with fresh produce. They mount everything on a bicycle and go to each house shouting out things for selling. Housewives who need those supplies come to the bicycle to select the goods they want and pay the seller on the spot. This means that my friends who were living in this high-rise had to head downstairs every time they wanted to buy something.

The clever system they had found involved tying a rope to a plastic basket, which they would send down when the fish monger or vegetable seller came. They would yell what they wanted from the sixth floor, and the seller would weigh it and put it into the basket.

My friend's wife would then pull up the rope and it would bring the basket with the supplies up. She would then empty the basket, put in the money, and then follow the same process to send down the basket. Apparently, everyone in such apartment complexes was doing the same. This is a simple system, but it served the purpose well.

Sometimes what we need are very simple systems.

Applying this principle to the products we design tells us that sometimes what we need are very simple systems. Therefore, it is important that we invest our time and effort into building simple yet powerful designs with the potential to accommodate future changes.

We may have seen engineering teams trying to build complex designs meant to solve simple problems. By all means, building good designs is really smart, but we have to keep asking the question, "Is there a way to simplify this?" This is a challenge to engineers and technical teams. In software engineering, we have seen pioneer architectural designs, like micro services, emerging after taking this into account. Similarly, in a problem-solving environment, we need to find ways to simplify the design and build more fluid systems, so that future changes can be easily accommodated.

10. Simplicity, the art of maximizing the amount of work not done, is essential.

Unused product features

I am sure you have either used Microsoft Word or at least heard about it. This word processor has been an aid for most people over the years, from students to corporate officers and beyond.

Ever since its first release, this software has evolved significantly. With every release it introduces many features that are of real help to many professionals. Starting from spelling and grammar checks, to paragraph formatting and word art, various features have proven really useful. However, I should confess I am unfamiliar with some of the features and their functionalities. I am sure there are some people more familiar with many more of the features of this software, but as an average user, I really don't need all these features. I just need very basic functions.

But really, how many features are available on Microsoft Word that I don't know? Below is a count of the 2013 version's listed features:

Table 1: Number of features in Microsoft word 2003

Menu/Toolbar Name	No of Items Listed
File menu	46
Edit menu	26
View menu	44
Insert menu	45
Format menu	31
Tools menu	52
Table menu	37
Window menu	5
Help menu	9
Standard toolbar	46
Formatting toolbar	48
AutoText toolbar	3
Control Toolbox toolbar	15
Database toolbar	10
Drawing toolbar	285
E-mail toolbar	41
Extended Formatting toolbar	10
Forms toolbar	13
Frames toolbar	7
Function Key Display toolbar	12
Ink Annotations	8
Ink Drawing and Writing toolbar	7

Japanese Greetings toolbar	7
Mail Merge toolbar	32
Outlining toolbar	22
Picture toolbar	24
Reviewing toolbar	25
Tables and Borders toolbar	36
Visual Basic toolbar	9
Web toolbar	16
Web Tools toolbar	16
Word Count toolbar	2
WordArt toolbar	10
3-D Settings toolbar	70
Shadow Settings toolbar	48
Drawing Canvas toolbar	12
Organization Chart toolbar	21
Diagram toolbar	31
Header and Footer toolbar	18
Full Screen toolbar	1
Stop Recording toolbar	4
Microsoft toolbar	8
Print Preview toolbar	10
AutoSummarize toolbar	3
Exit Design Mode toolbar	1
Text Box toolbar	6
Refresh toolbar	2
Reading Layout toolbar	14
Compare Side by Side toolbar	3
System toolbar	6
Online Meeting toolbar	7
============================	====
TOTAL Items	1264

Have you used all of these features? Personally, I have used only 8 to 10 percent of them. As for the rest of the features, I did not even know they existed. I was just wondering how much effort has been spent on building these features that customers do not often use (which remains a question for Microsoft).

However, this is not that different from most of the software or products we build. We create and offer many features, and customers do not even have an idea what their function is.

Why do we build it if it's not used?

According to research done by the Standish Group, only 20 percent of features of custom-developed applications are used. That means 80 percent of features are rarely or hardly used. This is pretty much aligned with what I have experienced in product development. We spend more time and effort building features which add hardly any value to the product. Sometimes, customers demand some features thinking they might be necessary, but they do not state any rationale behind why those features might be required, let alone how much value these particular features would deliver.

FEATURES USED

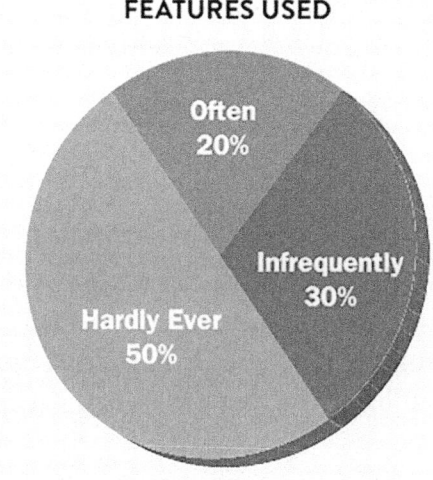

The Standish Group estimate of features used in custom application development.

Figure 7: Software product feature usage (Standish group, 2013)

That is why we need to think twice before we start the process of building anything. We need to consider carefully how these processes cost time and money.

Economical way

Building any product or product feature takes time, money, and effort. After spending so much effort, if the product or the feature created does not deliver any value, then the effort ends up being sheer waste. That money could have been spent to generate some other product of value. It is, therefore, important to prioritize product features before we commit to spending more money and time on them.

Customers who want only the most important product features get their value more quickly. They also get to pay only for the most important product features. They do not end up spending money on less sellable product features or product features they hardly use.

From the standpoint of the development team, it allows them to spend their efforts on the most important product features, and they are more motivated to solve the problems most important to the customers.

Practices

Agile has a few practices that promote this principle, including creation of product backlog, product backlog prioritization based on value, writing user stories, and product backlog and so on. These practices are helpful when it comes to delivering economic value to the customer and utilizing the best efforts of the team.

11. The best architectures, requirements, and designs emerge from self-organizing teams.

Steve Jobs once said, "You should not hire smart people and tell them what to do." I recall my experience as a team member, and I became very frustrated when my managers started micro-managing me and telling me how I should do my work. We were a team of software engineers and once we finished writing the code and testing it, he asked us to approach his desk, where he went through all of our codes and started re-writing them as he pointed out mistakes. From the time he called us to his desk around 4.30 pm, we could not leave the office until around 7 pm when he completed re-writing the code. Each of us had to go through that process, and it was not a good experience to see this team leader erase our code and re-write it as he reminded us of how crappy the code was, and how much more brilliantly he could re-write it. The organization did not have any coding standards, and so each of us had done what we were used to. His reiterations affected each of us very negatively. It was demotivating.

We did not warrant any lecturers on how crappy our work was, but we remained open-minded about what we should have done to improve. Nevertheless, the way the team leader went about correcting us diminished our creativity and spirit. I left the company within six weeks, and the rest of my colleagues followed same. After just a few years, that company went bankrupt. This experience has convinced me that he was the kind of boss I do not want to ever work with in my life.

We make the biggest mistakes as coaches or managers by directing our employees on how to carry out their jobs. Rather, we should give them a purpose and they will find the best way to do the job. That has been proven in all of the management projects in which I have been involved.

SELF-ORGANIZED TEAMS WITH AUTONOMY

As mentioned earlier, in management we create self-organized teams, build an environment, give them a mission or product vision, and set the teams free. We give them autonomy, and by doing so, they come up with the best strategies, best architectures, best designs, and best methods on how to do things. This is because they are more intelligent and powerful than we think. It is their own small set-up and they have to find a way to be smart with it.

I recall one of the mining companies I coached as it went through business transformation. This particular project team consisted of geologists, geophysicists, and reservoir engineers. The product they were working on was to determine where the oil well should be drilled within the deep waters. The project involved a series of varied data point calculations and predictive analytics. Although the team used their internal tools as expected, they also went ahead and collected data from other regional data centers, yet no one, not even the senior manager, had asked them to do so. The way this team worked for two weeks with complete autonomy and self-organization blew the senior managers' minds. The senior manager had previously worked with them on a daily basis, telling them what to do. He believed this team was not mature enough to determine how to their job, so he was used to directing them and telling them what to do and how to do it. However, this time around as part of Agile transformation, senior managers were not allowed to interfere with their teams, and instead teams were given full autonomy and accountability. That specific team made managers realize that evidently, teams are indeed capable of doing things the best way possible.

This demonstrates that what leaders need to do in management is to let teams enjoy their autonomy and solve impediments as they arise. Somehow a team will find a way to do its job.

12. At regular intervals, the team reflects on how to become more effective, then tunes and adjusts its behavior accordingly.

Figure 8 : Resisting continuous improvement

Continuous improvement

In one of the SAFe Agile trainings, one of the senior leaders aired his view about Agile as, "This is some old shit by a new name." Actually, he was correct. Most of us do the same things under a new name or banner. The core things we did or the way we worked never change. If we continue to carry out useless practices that we used to do in the traditional development process, Agile is going to be the same old stuff.

That is why continuous improvement is mandatory in any Agile project. In every setup, there are things that work and things that do not work. Any organization has that. But in order to continue running the organization profitably, it must work on continuous improvements.

Team Decides.

Well, any organization can identify and implement continuous improvements. What is so different in Agile? The answer is simple. The team identifies what needs to be improved and they implement it. This is the major difference between the continuous improvements by Agile teams and improvements in the traditional and other systems.

Most organizations force changes or productivity improvements on teams. Management decides which improvement is needed and enforces it. As a result, the team feels unappreciated and redundant, and they no longer take ownership when it comes to improvements being made. Ultimately, the demanded changes cannot really succeed.

This is not the case in Agile teams. Teams do work together for a long time, as they chase a common goal. When doing so, some things work for the better while some do not, which means they are the very best people suited to identify what works for them and what does not. And they are also the best placed to discuss and agree on what to do and how to go around what is not working.

Agile practices

Agile practices are implemented using regular retrospectives in the Agile process. The team looks back and identifies what has not been working, and they then come up with plans to correct the problems and implement better strategies. That is how teams become high performers over a period of time.

Summary

In this chapter we have surveyed the Agile principles, which play a major role in identifying how and why Agile practices are implemented. They make clear the rationale behind the manner of doing things. A scrum master requires this knowledge, and even deeper, on how Agile principles work, as he or she is the change agent and the mentor to the team and the organization.

CHAPTER 6

Agile frameworks

A GILE IS BECOMING a new way of delivering value to businesses and customers. In fact, it has been heavily applied in Information Technology companies, and non-IT companies have lately begun to join the journey by adopting Agile. Some of the companies that have embraced Agile are big multinationals.

IBM embraces Agile

One such organization is IBM, a company famous for its processes. IBM has adopted Agile in most of its internal processes, and for the period I worked there almost all IBM subsidiaries had adopted Agile in its projects delivery and also offered Agile as a service to its clients. For example, I helped IBM customers initiate Agile transformations by coaching them and providing leadership.

Former Chief Innovation Officer (CIO) of IBM, Jeff Smith, played a huge role in Agile adaptation in IBM, and he explained in one of his interviews how 400,000 employees can be 40,000 squads of ten self-organized team members instead of commanding and controlling individual employees. The CIO helped to cultivate the Agile culture at IBM. (c.f. youtube.com, How Jeff Smith built an Agile culture at IBM, minute 0.25)

3M Adopts Agile.

3M is another company that surprised me with its adaptation of Agile. I worked for 3M for five years, and during my time, and even before that, 3M was always a process-oriented company. It depended heavily on Six Sigma as a process improvement methodology, and based on their Six Sigma dependency, I never thought they would go anywhere near Agile. But I was wrong. This digital disruption will not let any organization remain isolated.

Recently, 3M started investing in Agile, and within two years the company's health information systems launched more than ninety Agile teams. This is a significant change considering how big and diverse these teams are.

Some other companies that have adopted Agile include SAP, Accenture, ING Direct, and British Petroleum (BP). It is difficult to find any company that has not started using Agile in some capacity.

One size does not fit all.

One thing to note is that these companies are completely different from one another. If I compare the companies for which I've worked, including Emirates Air lines, 3M, Massive Interactive, IBM, Accenture, and Cognizant (I excluded client companies like Channel NINE, Channel SEVEN, DBS Bank, NBN Australia, and BP), it's clear they are totally different in terms of business models, types of products, size of company (in terms of revenue, market share, and number of employees), and geographical expansion.

All of them have adopted Agile as of now, although some of them joined the journey much later. I am happy for them as they have had the courage to accept the inevitable. As an employee who worked for them some time back, and as an Agile transformation leader, and now a coach, there is one thing that is clear to me: one Agile framework does not fit all organizations. This is applicable to other companies out in the market as well.

Every company is different, with various products, goals, and operating models. How would it be possible for one framework to fit all of them? Luckily, Agile has many frameworks from which to choose. Depending on the complexity of the systems, problems, and goals, these frameworks can be wisely selected. As a scrum master, you need to have some good understanding of these frameworks, but to my surprise, some scrum masters have not even heard of the frameworks I have listed below, except 'scrum.'

Why a Scrum Master should know these frameworks

Most scrum masters started their journey with a scrum framework. This is the simplest framework we have seen and it is a good starting point. But if your organization decides to implement SAFe as the framework, then the scrum master should be able to quickly adjust and help to implement it. Although most of the fundamentals remain the same, a scrum master should be able to understand the chosen and at least speak the same language. For example, a scrum master should not be surprised to hear the phrase 'PI planning.'

I have seen scrum masters who are knowledgeable in only one framework, and such scrum masters try to implement the framework they know within another framework or sometimes they do not adopt the practices of the new framework, thereby putting the entire Agile transformation at risk. For instance, if your organization is using Large Scale Scrum (LeSS) as the framework and you are the scrum master of a one squad framework, you should be able to represent your squad at scrum of scrum events. If you resist scrum of scrum events, it may arouse conflict among all squads. Basically, as the scrum master you must be conscious about whatever practices you have in your framework and what your role is within that practice.

Apart from adhering to the practices, your knowledge on different frameworks can be helpful to the organization when it comes to selecting the right framework. As a scrum master, then, you should bring a genuine interest in other frameworks and expand your knowledge beyond the framework with which you are most familiar – for the benefit of both yourself and the organization.

Different Frameworks

There are many Agile frameworks, and each is applied in one organization or another. Some organizations use one framework in their Human Resources department while using a different framework in their IT departments.

Below is a list of such frameworks that have proven widely popular among different organizations.

- Disciplined Agile 2.0
- Dynamic Systems Development Method (DSDM), now referred to as Framework for Business Agility
- Enterprise Scrum
- Fast Agile Scaled Technology (FAST)
- Large-Scale Scrum (LeSS)
- Nexus
- Recipes for Agile Governance in the Enterprise (RAGE)
- Scaled Agile Framework (SAFe) 4.5
- ScALeD Agile Lean Development (ScALeD)
- Scrum at Scale
- Spotify
- eXponential Simple Continuous Autonomous Learning Ecosystem (XSCALE)

We recommend getting a grasp of these frameworks, even if ultimately it will be your choice to stick with one framework and master it. For example, I have met Agile coaches who say, "I am convinced Large Scale Scrum is the best and do not want to coach other frameworks." Choosing the framework to work with is a personal preference based on the perceptions, knowledge, career goals and probably many other reasons.

The aim of this book is not to provide deep theoretical knowledge on Agile frameworks, but for the reader's benefit I provide a high level of details of some of the popular Agile frameworks in the chapters that follow.

Scrum Framework

Scrum is the simplest framework. According to *The Scrum Guide*, "Scrum is a simple framework for effective team collaboration on complex software projects" (www.Scrum.org, 2018). I believe most scrum masters studied scrum framework in the person's early career stages. Since it is a common and popular framework, I will not spend time explaining it here, but I would direct readers to *The Scrum Guide* which is available online free of charge for further details. Scrum guide has been co-authored by its co-creators, Ken Schwaber and Jeff Sutherland.

Figure 9: Jeff Sutherland(left) and Ken Schwaber(right)
(Scrum.org, 2018)

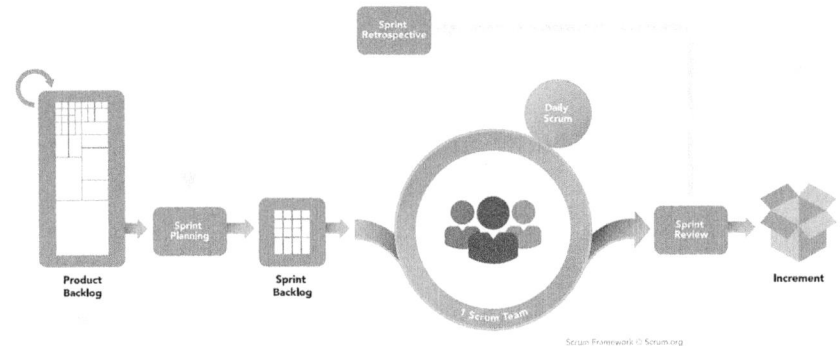

Figure 10: SCRUM framework (Scrum.org)

To download *The Scrum Guide*, visit https://www.scrum.org/ resources/scrum-guide

Where it is applicable

Scrum framework is applicable in almost any product development environment. All software development projects in which I have been involved have used the scrum framework at the team level. It can be applied anywhere, and one example is the oil and gas company I mentioned earlier, which started its Agile journey with this framework. Before scaling it, they wanted to try it out by hosting a pilot project, and for this purpose they selected the scrum framework since it is the simplest of all. After seeing the success of scrum, they decided to roll it out globally. They had been skeptical about it at the beginning because they were not implementing it on IT projects but with pure oil and gas projects such as digging of oil wells. However, success of those scrum pilots was phenomenal, proving that the scrum framework can be applied even for specific industries.

Large Scale Scrum (LESS)

Why scaling SCRUM?

Large Scale Scrum comes into the picture when Agile principles need to be applied at scale. This makes more sense as scrum at team level, which is the grass root level, works in most organizations. Unlike small start-ups, most of the organizations using Agile are large and have many employees. They need to have multiple teams working together to produce a given piece of work or product.

That is why we need to scale Scrum to a larger degree.

Problems solved by LeSS

In the process of developing products, I have been involved with anywhere from twenty to fifty team members in any given situation. Although the group was developing a single product, the team members may be spread out over different geographical locations. For example, I have had people from India, Pakistan, Vietnam, Philippines, China, Poland, United Kingdom, and Canada on my teams. Regardless of where we were based, however, we were able to work together as one. But the truth is, hundreds of teams are too large to operate as a single team. Communication, geographical barriers, cultural barriers, and personality differences all add complexities and contribute to longer value delivery cycles. In our case, we lost transparency, productivity, and team bonding due those differences.

Team complaints

There is a common complaint by Agile team members operating in large organizations, and that is, "There is no point in doing Agile. The rest of the organization is too slow or anti-Agile, so there is no point in being fast." This is what most of my teams who have operated using the scrum framework in larger organizations said.

Scrum teams make quick decisions and move quickly; however,

they lose momentum the moment they interact with other teams who are not operating in Agile because they find those other teams too slow for them. It is like one wheel of a car rotating swiftly while the other three are slow. The car must, inevitably, lose speed.

LeSS addresses this challenge by applying scrum to more than one team and allowing it to be synchronized towards one common goal.

LeSS

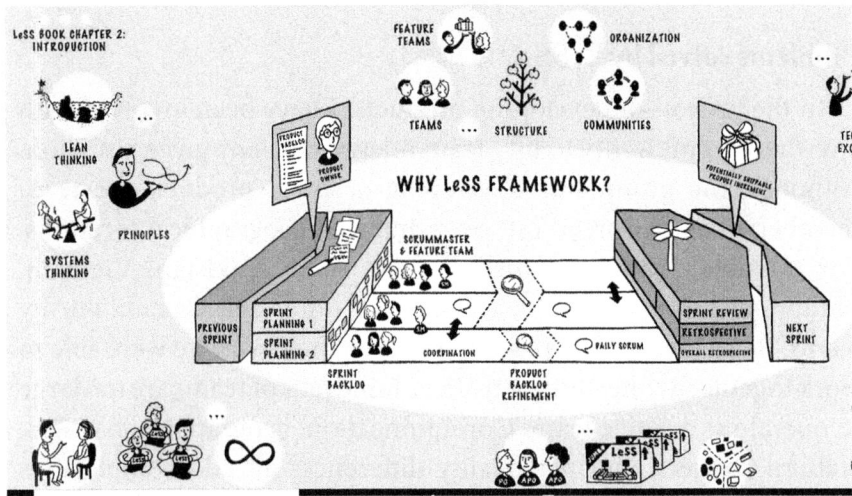

Figure 11 : LeSS Framework (Less.works)

LeSS Principles

Similar to the Agile principles, LeSS builds on a solid set of parameters as listed below.

- Large scale scrum is scrum.
- Empirical process control.

- Transparency.
- More with less.
- Whole product focus.
- Customer Centric.
- Continuous improvement towards perfection.
- Systems thinking.
- Lean thinking.
- Queuing theory.

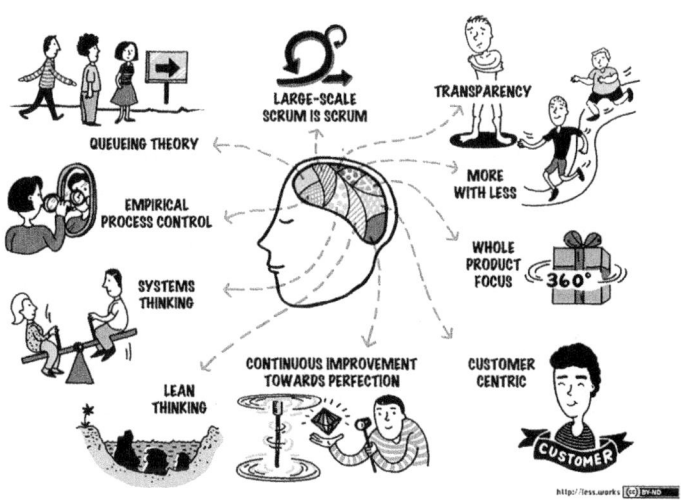

Figure 12 : LeSS principles (Less.works)

Read up on these principles at the LeSS website. https://less.works/less/principles/overview.html

How LeSS is structured

LeSS is structured around multiple teams operating on Agile values, principles, and practices. Each individual team consists of scrum master(s), product owner(s), and a development team. LeSS practices help align self-organized teams toward a common goal of developing a single product.

The principles call for aligning two to eight teams, or more, to deliver one single product. Each team consists of three to nine people, and all teams have one product backlog. There are also designated feature teams, each being self-organized, and all solving inter-dependencies on their own, as opposed to solutions coming down from the scrum master or the product owner. The goal of all teams is to ship working software at the end of the sprint.

They sometimes must jump onto one another's team to help finish off the work since all of them have the same goal.

LeSS Rules

For the implementation purpose, LeSS has proposed few rules as listed here:

- Sprint planning consists of two parts, namely, Sprint planning 1 and 2.
- Sprint planning 1 is for the entire product. Representatives from all teams attend this event and get clarity on the product features.
- Sprint planning 2 happens after sprint planning 1 which is conducted at team level.
- Teams select the product features based on the priority setup of the product owner.
- If required, the teams negotiate and swap the product features in a way that makes best use of the sprint time and provide utmost product value.
- In sprint planning 1, teams identify dependencies, establish who is working on what items, and also clarify final questions from one another and from the product owner.

- Each team must create its own sprint backlog by breaking down the product features they choose into workable user stories/tasks.

- Prefers decentralization and informal coordination among teams and team members.

- Perfection rule is to improve the definition of 'Done,' which results in a shippable product after every sprint or even more frequently.

- Team retrospectives are done at each team level at the end of each sprint, and these identify improvements required at the team level.

- Group retrospectives are done at the end of each sprint with representatives from every teams. This is an important event as it helps all teams to identify the improvements required when working as one group.

- Teams identify ways to coordinate among themselves.

- Teams do multi-team and/or overall products backlog refinement to increase shared understanding. This expands opportunities for cross-team coordination, especially when there are items which require group leaning or collective problem solving.

- Although teams do the product backlog refinements, it is the product owner who decides prioritization.

- Only one sprint review per product at the end of the sprint is conducted.

The video below a good summary of LeSS framework:
https://www.youtube.com/watch?v=e7mzpKHOAHs

Large LeSS.

Large LeSS is the second part of the LeSS framework. When a product development requires more than eight teams, Large LeSS can be applied. It is best suited to apply Scrum at large enterprise level. For further details, refer to the LeSS website or talk to a LeSS consultant.

References

Craig Larman, Bas Vodde, 2016,Large Scale Scrum, More with Less , Addison-Wesley

Kanban

Kanban is the easiest framework to implement as it is the simplest workflow management system. When multiple jobs are there to be managed, Kanban can be easily applied.

Pull system

Kanban is a pull system, meaning production starts when a customer places an order. When the product is delivered, production stops. This helps eliminate wasteful production and avoid building an inventory of products not required by the customers.

Three simple things

Kanban only needs three simple things to implement:

- Board
- List
- Card

Board

Board is the workflow. Just like in a manufacturing plant, the board has many workflows. For example, a car is assembled at many different workstations, and each workstation does a unique job like putting on tires or assembling the doors.

In the Agile environment, the board is the presentation of those workflows. If we apply this in a normal workplace, human resources, sales, and finance are different workflows, hence acting as the boards.

Figure 13: Kanban Board

List

The list represents different parts of the production line (workstations). In normal Kanban implementation, a list is a lane through which each item is supposed to through. They are simply column headers:

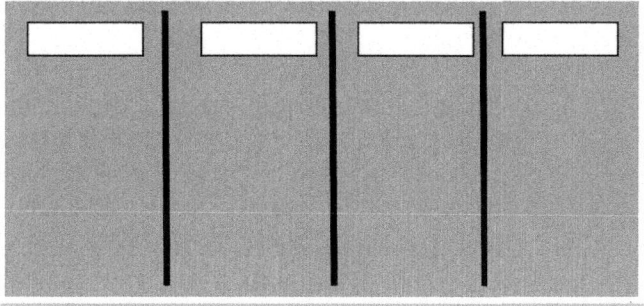

Figure 14: Lists

Card

Card represents the work item. As the work progresses, the work item moves along the production line, with different people in the production line working on the item at different times.

Day 1

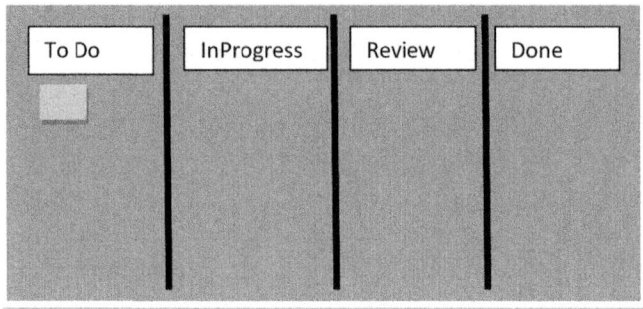

Figure 15: Cards

Day 2

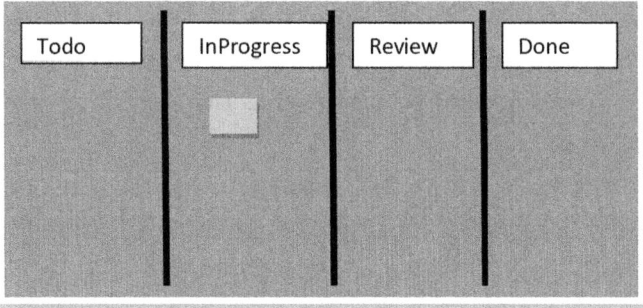

For example, above is a simple Kanban board for a credit card application process. The list of applications, Appl1, Appl 2, and so on, will be in the queue, what is essentially the backlog, and the teams that specialize in document verifications, approval, and card issuing will pull each of the applications as per their capacity. For instance, App 2 has been pulled by the Document Verification Team and is in progress as per the above board. When it is finished, the Approval Team can pull that application when they have capacity.

As is clear, this simplest of formats can be implemented by anyone, any department, or any IT development. This visual representation of work emits much information from the work items, such as where the work item is, who is working on it, and what other work is pending.

Application of Kanban.

In enterprise organizations, Kanban can be applied anywhere. For example, if you are in the marketing department, you can have a Kanban board that represents the work you are supposed to have.

I remember Jimmy Ng who implemented Kanban in his audit department of DBS bank–Singapore. "Kanban is the simplest format we could implement, and it has brought us a lot of productivity improvement in our audit department," Jimmy reported. (Jimmy NG, 2017).

Scaled Agile FRAMEWORK (SAFe)

Scaled Agile Framework (SAFe) is my favorite framework. This framework connects all the layers of an organization, and if applied correctly, it has the potential to reduce waste across the value stream of an entire organization.

There is a reason for my bias. My experience is mostly with global and regional companies where I was accountable for overall project delivery. Almost all of those programs or projects, in both regional and global organizations, involved teams/partners/suppliers from different countries and spanned a few years. Traditional project management is time consuming and effortful, and that is why Agile is a perfect fit.

Applying agile at scale

If agile can be scaled to fit such larger teams, then it can really help deliver benefits. That is where Scaled Agile comes in, as it combines lean and agile principles and aligns strategic missions into operations. If we can make the strategy transparent across all the layers of the organization and make all teams work with autonomy, value delivery within the organization would be more effective, and we could drastically reduce waste. That is what SAFe does in an enterprise.

In my experience, it is the most successful framework in the corporate world where several hundred people, sometimes thousands, work toward a common goal and with common passion. This is not to say that SAFe is perfect. In fact, it is always evolving, going through an empirical development cycle in any organization, thus improving along the way.

What is most admired about SAFe is its clear and precise implementation roadmap, which starts from the leadership layer. Most of the organizations do fail in the Agile adoption because leadership is not aligned with Agile values and principles. When we implement Agile, we see that teams do quickly adapt to it, but management may not, so the organization cannot reap the full benefits as expected from such transformation. For this reason, SAFe starts from the leadership team and trains them on adopting the Agile mindset, principles, and practices. This sequence helps build the right environment for the Agile teams, enabling them to be fully autonomous.

SAFe Values.

SAFe framework is built on four core values

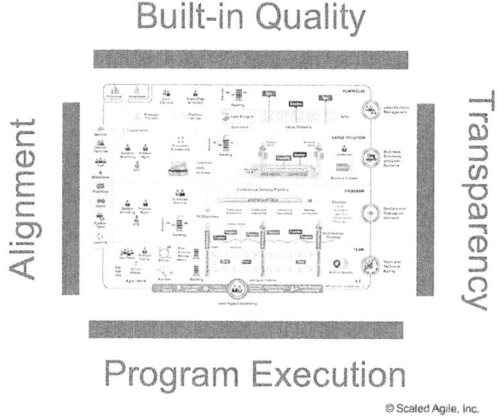

Figure 16 : SAFe core values (Scaledagileframwework.com)

Alignment

Organizations naturally go through many changes, especially due to external demands, and customers need different things; changes occur that call for the organizations that provide these products or services to be sensitive to these changes. In fact, they are expected to realign themselves and deliver what customers ask for.

Organizations do this by adjusting their strategies, but it is important that when the strategy is adjusted and changed, this quickly reflects across the rest of the organization. The question is, does this happen and are the strategic changes supported?

SAFe framework connects all layers of the organization. Prioritizing the strategic themes is done by considering the economic value and then the enterprise solutions layer plans the value stream using Agile principles. Those value streams are then realized using one or more solutions train engines (program of works). Those solutions are then delivered by program teams that operate in an Agile environment using Agile principles and practices. Production teams build nothing apart from what is required in order to deliver the strategic themes.

Build in Quality.

A long time ago when I was in software development, testing was done at the end of the development process, to make sure that software development met the client's requirements. It was the last thing to be done and development teams hated it most of the time. As a result of the testing, bugs or defects would be found and that meant developers had to fix them quickly and have retesting done before the software could be deployed. That resulted in late hours and sometimes working weekends.

This is why we need to ensure we build quality right from the beginning. When the quality is integrated and built from the first line of code, there is no longer needed to do quality assurance at the end of the development process.

SAFe explains this as illustrated below. Quality is inbuilt at every step of the development process, whether code, integration, release, or architecture.

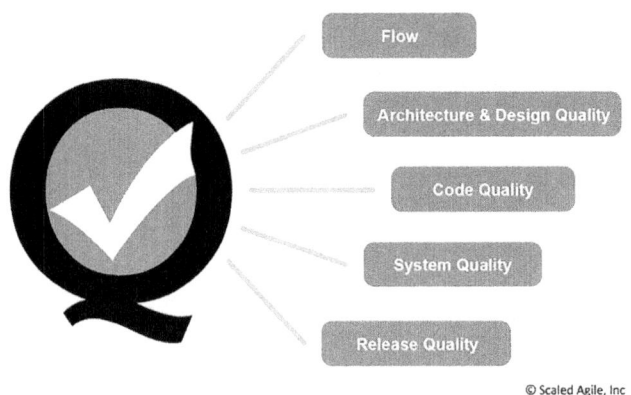

© Scaled Agile, Inc

Figure 17: SAFe build in quality (Scaledagileframework.com)

Transparency.

Transparency is one of the main values of SAFe. From top to bottom, transparency is maintained within the enterprise. Transparency helps build trust and transmit information so that decision making becomes easy.

There are many SAFe practices that encourage transparency. For example, Program Increment (PI) planning is one big event that makes transparent strategic decisions, dependencies, and team confidence.

Program execution.

Program execution involves many teams working toward a common goal and using Agile principles to deliver valuable product/service at the strategic level. Teams need to work together, to be synchronized, and to support one another rather than working alone as silos. SAFe supports this mindset. SAFe Agile Release Trains (ART) align multiple Agile teams who follow the same cadence. This is applying Agile at the program level, at the very least, but when larger initiatives are being executed and therefore there are multiple programs being executed using the same practice and principles, it focuses on the entire value stream rather than just one portion of the value stream.

SAFe Principles

Built upon SAFe values, SAFe stands on the principles listed below:

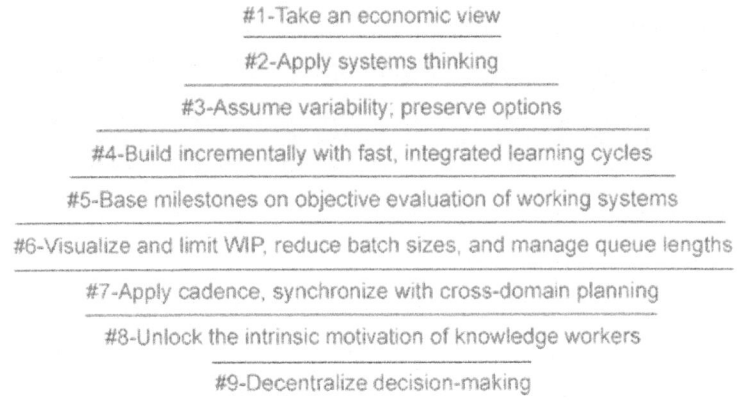

#1-Take an economic view

#2-Apply systems thinking

#3-Assume variability; preserve options

#4-Build incrementally with fast, integrated learning cycles

#5-Base milestones on objective evaluation of working systems

#6-Visualize and limit WIP, reduce batch sizes, and manage queue lengths

#7-Apply cadence, synchronize with cross-domain planning

#8-Unlock the intrinsic motivation of knowledge workers

#9-Decentralize decision-making

Figure 18: SAFe Principles (Scaledagileframework.com)

These SAFe principles are well explained in all SAFe trainings.

Leading SAFe is a training which gives leaders a good understanding of how to lead a SAFe implementation. They need to cultivate a leadership mindset especially around the concept of giving autonomy to the team. During this training, we normally explain these SAFe principles, and almost all the leaders agree that these SAFe principles indeed make sense.

For example, 'applying systems thinking' involves removing isolated problem-solving and helping optimize the entire value stream.

For detailed explanation on these SAFe principles, refer to the SAFe website: https://www.scaledagileframework.com/safe-lean-agile-principles/

How SAFe is structured.

As at the time of writing this book, SAFe had released its newest version SAFe 4.6. SAFe 4.6 is structured into four levels as listed below:

- SAFe portfolio
- SAFe solution
- SAFe Program
- SAFe Teams

All four layers are called Full SAFe, and all of them are applied in big enterprises to help plan the strategic investments/initiatives as portfolios using lean Agile principles.

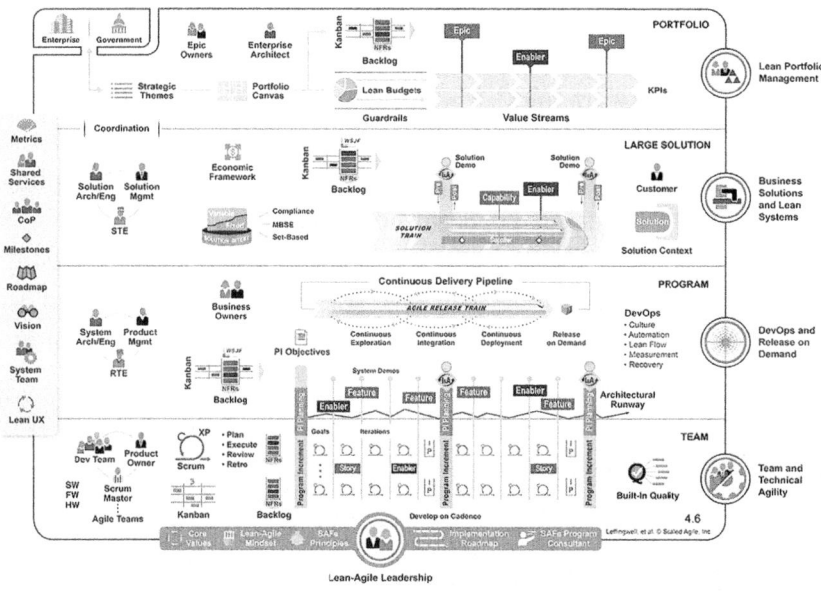

Figure 19: SAFe levels (Scaledagileframework.com)

SAFe Portfolio.

SAFe portfolio level helps to apply lean Agile principles at the strategic, enterprise level of the organization. It helps to respond to external changes like economic or government regulations and internal changes like reorganizations. This layer helps in planning the strategy of the organization by using strategic themes or initiatives.

Prioritizing those strategic themes based on the economic value and best outcomes are essential features of this layer. Such strategic themes are implemented using single or multiple solutions.

SAFe Solution.

Strategic themes are implemented using large solutions. For example, if the strategic theme is to gain 10 percent of the market share within two years, this strategy may be implemented using a multiple-solution plan, such as, new customer relationship management software, new product portfolio, or new sales training program. These solutions should be interlinked and working as one solution to deliver the strategic goals. If the solutions are applied individually, the strategic goals cannot be realized.

SAFe solution involves helping organize these solutions using lean Agile principles. New roles at this level are introduced as Solutions Train Engineers (STE), Solutions Architects, and Solutions managers.

Each solution is implemented using one of multiple programs known as Agile Release Trains (ART).

SAFe Program layer

SAFe program layer implements solutions identified at the solutions layer. The programs themselves are called release train engines, and one or more release trains may be required to deliver a solution. Each release train engine delivers a product increment for every program increment, which is normally within eight to ten weeks.

Just imagine that a new strategic intuitive is identified and it is prioritized, and then one consumable part is delivered within the next three months. Considering the way traditional development delivers work, this new way of working is fast, responds to change, and has a high competitive advantage. As I mentioned, if SAFe is implemented correctly, it can deliver significant results to the company and to its customers.

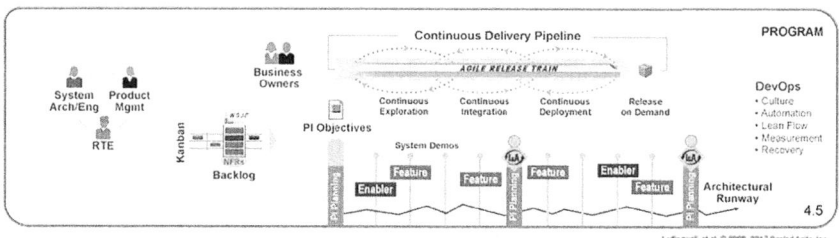

Figure 20: SAFe Program layer (Scaledagileframwork.com)

SAFe Teams.

Each release train or program increment is implemented by multiple Agile teams which use either Scrum or Kanban. These teams are autonomous and put Agile principles into practice.

As a scrum master, this is where your involvement is maximized. You are expected to play a role within the scrum team as well as within the program layer, especially during the event called Program Increment (PI) planning.

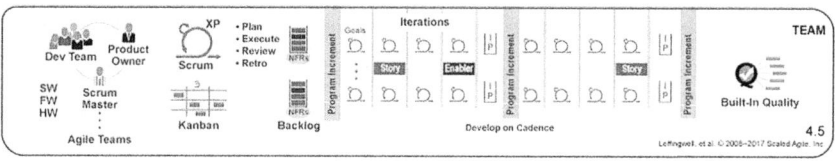

Figure 21: SAFe Team layer (Scaledagileframwork.com)

SAFe Training.

As scrum master (if you happen to use this framework), you are expected to understand how SAFe works, its values and principles, and support the product owner and the team to adopt the SAFe framework. Strong servant leadership is required during the PI planning and then when executing the cadence once PI planning is completed. More knowledge in this area is essential, and so attending a SAFe Scrum Master training session is certainly worth the time.

References

Richard Knaster and Dean Leffingwell, 2018,SAFe 4.5 Distilled: Applying the Scaled Agile Framework for Lean Software and Systems Engineering

ScaledAgileframework.com, (2019), Retrieved 30 July, 2019, from https://www.scaledagileframework.com/

Spotify

When we talk about experiencing music, there are two major companies that revolutionized how music is experienced. The first is Apple and the other is Spotify.

Apple introduced the iPod which stored thousands of songs, changing the way we experience music. Before that we used portable music players, but these would store only a few songs compared to the thousands of songs one could store on an iPod.

Spotify, on the other hand, had with a different strategy. Instead of storing songs on the device, Spotify used the internet to store songs, then offered streaming as a service. Unlike Apple, Spotify is device-independent and available on almost any platform as long as there is an internet connection (and higher subscription prices allow offline storage as well).

From 2006 to 2018, Spotify has grown to have 3,000 employees, and it has 170 million users, 75 million of them being paying customers. In 2017, the company generated €4.09 billion in revenue (Wikipediaorg. (2019). This is significant growth for a new business model that was unique at the time the company started. How did Spotify achieve this success? Among the many factors that contributed to its meteoric rise, such as leadership and a new business model, their product development framework should be given credit for that success. They call this framework "Spotify."

Spotify model

Spotify has a unique organizational structure. It is a flat structure with minimal hierarchies, and the focus is on autonomous, self-organized teams. These small teams are called "Squads."

Structure of Spotify framework

Spotify is structured around squads, tribes, chapters, and guilds. Let us examine this framework in detail so that the reader understands where he or she would sit and what the responsibilities would be if acting as scrum master in one of those squads.

The **Squad** is the smallest unit that is responsible for the start to the end of a solution. These units do have a mission, as they provide a solution and take the ownership of that solution even after it goes live. It works like a mini start-up and runs like a business. They are self-sufficient in terms of resources, and they make their own decisions on how to run their own business. They take pride if their solution is successful and learn from it if it fails. Failure is nothing to be scared of as it is a learning experience.

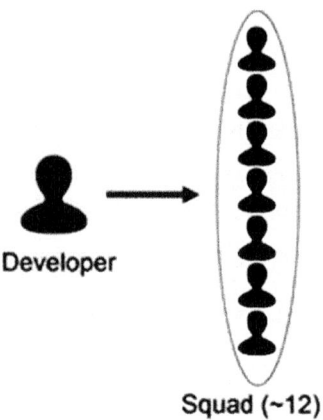

Figure 22: Squad

Squad consists of six to twelve members, comprising UX designers, researchers, developers, testers, and other experts. All have equal rights and hold an equal position in terms of hierarchy. Squad has a flat hierarchy and its leader is a servant leader who uses a similar skill set as a scrum master. That means facilitating stand-ups, showcases, helping the product owner refine the product backlog, coaching, and helping the team get impediments resolved.

The team itself decides how to operate. This means it is up to them whether to use scrum or Kanban or extreme programming. There is only one consideration for them and that is, "What works for the team?" Once they agree on what that is, they implement it. After some time, if they realize their chosen way of working is not productive, and if they are indeed unanimous about it, they switch to another one. They make decisions and take responsibility for the success or failure.

Tribes

Squads are grouped on a theme and are known as tribes. A tribe can have few squads like five to seven or more, and it is structured mostly on the basis of a product that they are building.

It can also be based on a solution they were building. For example, all CRM squads form a CRM tribe, and each squad of CRM could be developing and releasing a different feature of the final product, CRM. The features relevant to sales could be done by the 'Sales Squad' and features relevant to marketing done by the 'Marketing cloud.'

A tribe has a 'Tribe Leader' and usually he or she is an experienced 'Squad Leader' who has had the opportunity to work on one or more squads.

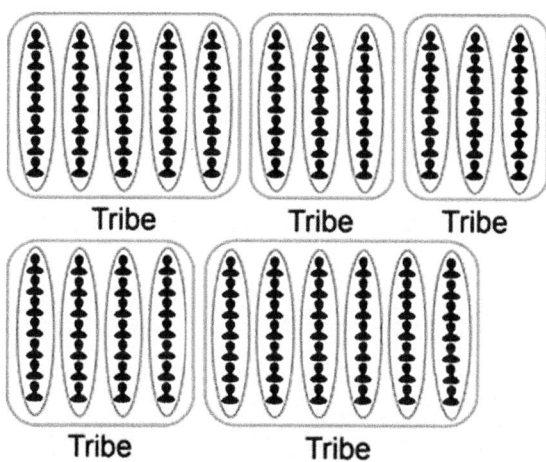

Figure 23: Tribes(Henrik Kniberg& Anders Ivarsson, 2012)

Chapter

A chapter consists of members with similar interests or skill set. For example, product owners can have their own chapter and UX designers can have their own chapter. It is similar to a community of practice (COP).

Chapters allow individuals to grow their knowledge and skills in their specific areas of practice. They may conduct trainings and share best practices and the like.

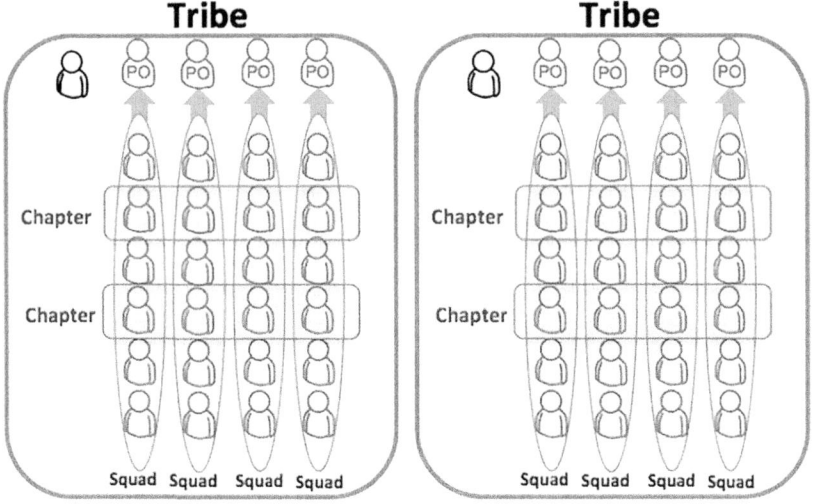

Figure 24 : Tribes (Henrik Kniberg& Anders Ivarsson, 2012)

Guild

A guild is a community of interest. People who want to share their interest and knowledge from different tribes can form guilds. It does not necessarily target individuals using that particular skill set, but he or she may just wish to learn it. For instance, a guild for 'public speaking' can be created, and anyone who would like to participate can be a member of that guild.

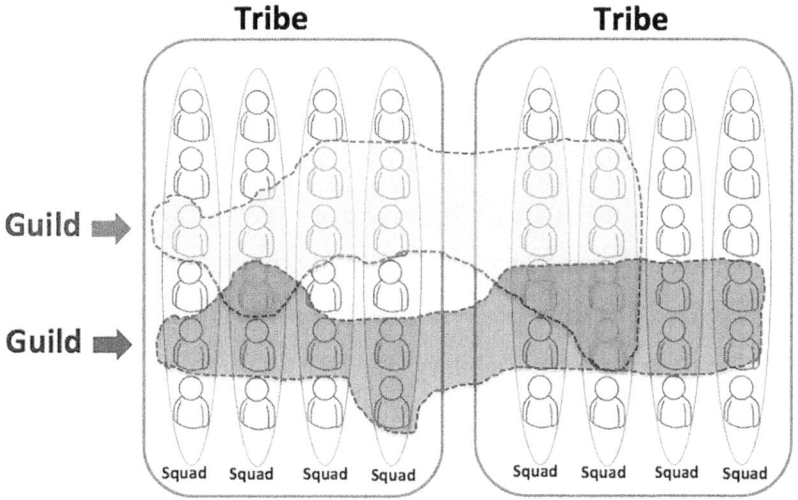

Figure 25: Guilds (Henrik Kniberg& Anders Ivarsson, 2012)

Scrum Master's Involvement

If you happen to be a scrum master in this framework, your involvement would mostly be at squad level. Apart from that, you may also qualify to be a tribe leader if you have excellent facilitation skills. Also, you can be a chapter lead for Scrum/Agile.

References

Scaling Agile @ Spotify , Henrik Kniberg& Anders Ivarsson, 2012
Wikipediaorg. (2019). Wikipediaorg. Retrieved 30 July, 2019, from https://en.wikipedia.org/wiki/Spotify

Other Agile frameworks

There are many other agile frameworks in the industry apart from those described above. Below is a list of those frameworks:

- Extreme Programming (XP)
- Crystal
- Feature Driven Development (FDD)
- Dynamic Systems Development Method (DSDM)
- Disciplined Agile Delivery (DAD)

These frameworks are also used in specific projects within the industry.

CHAPTER 7

Responsibilities of Scrum Master

K EN SCHWABER AND Jeff Sutherland are special people. They are the master minds behind the Scrum framework. According to them, Scrum is:

- Lightweight
- Simple to understand
- Difficult to master

(www.Scrum.org, 2018).

There is no better way than that to explain 'scrum,' and in my experience, this statement is true in every possible way. Scrum is the simplest framework but mastering it takes effort, passion, and dedication.

Most people think scrum, or let's say, Agile, is about stand-ups, sprint planning, and retrospectives, yet those are only a few of the activities in scrum. Scrum is much more than that. In the following chapters, we seek to understand more deeply the other aspects of scrum. When playing the role of 'scrum master,' what things does one need to do?

To facilitate the process answering the above question, the next three chapters treat in sequence the following separate concepts:
Responsibilities of the scrum master before the project

- Responsibilities of the scrum master during the project
- Responsibilities of the scrum master after the project

CHAPTER 8

Responsibilities of Scrum Master— Before the project start

THERE ARE MANY things to do before a project can really start, and handling some of these prerequisites will help you as well as your team. You may have to answer questions like the ones listed below before you can effectively embark on a project:

- What is the problem / business case of the project which your team needs to address?

- Why this project is starting?

- How is the project linked to the strategy or goals of the organization?

- Are there any milestones such as tradeshows, public events, or regulatory deadlines with which the project team needs to align?

- Is there a preferred framework they would like your team to work with or does the team have the autonomy to make their own choices?

- Has the team been selected? If so, where are the personnel located? Are they free of other project commitments? (Disregard this if you have been asked to select the team members.)

- Who are the stakeholders, those who will be impacted by the product you are developing? Does your team have to figure that out?

- Who is the product owner?

- Who is the point of contact to whom to deliver project details?

It's likely you may not have all of the answers, but each is worth asking. The process may give you a hint about the best place to begin.

Sometimes asking such questions provides a clue about whether it is advisable to take up this project or not, in cases of you contracting or starting a new job, in particular.

For instance, awhile back I was about to be hired as a scrum master, and when I asked about the product owner, I was told I had to play that role as well. The organization was new to Agile and I knew that many things needed to be done in order to start the project using Agile. I explained to that it is a recipe for failure. When they did not listen, I decided to decline the offer. Because many scrum masters are contractors, it would be worthwhile to get more clarity rather than taking up a project and then complaining about it later.

However, with a different client but in a similar situation, I was able to coach the hiring managers and the project sponsors and to identify a product owner allocated for the project. I explained to them that if they expected better results, they needed to have a dedicated product owner. They were serious about it because they wanted to propagate Agile to the rest of the organization, and they wanted things to start off on the right foot. If one wants to do a good job as scrum master, it is essential to get a good, clear picture of how you want to work before embarking on the project.

Once a clear picture is in focus, do the list of tasks below before starting the project.

Meet your team

The biggest strength and the most valuable resource you will have is your team. Without the team, a leader achieves little. Simon Sinek, who wrote the famous *Leaders Eat Last* book said, "Together is better." As scrum master, you should be able to build a team which is autonomous and self-organized, which means you must invest time mining the details about personnel, such as:

- Names
- Personalities
- Background
- Family (if they are willing to share)
- Agile experience
- Motivations
- Strengths /weaknesses
- Achievements
- Individual and team personality (more on this later)
- Skill set
- Activities outside of work for fun
- How they commute to work and where they live
- Previous projects
- Hobbies
- Prior experience working with these same team members
- Prior experience on any similar projects
- Special requirements
- How and what they like to learn

These are basic things a scrum master should know about the team and about every individual team member. The data can be collected either via formal meetings or by having informal catch-ups like a walk and talk or coffee. The choice on how to go about it is yours.

The important point to remember is that **you are a servant leader**. Command and control are things one must drop when taking the position of scrum master, in favor of working with the above information—the little details that will bring success at this job. For example, if one of your team members is an introvert, then you need to be smart, empathetic, and sensitive when trying to engage him or her in the retrospectives. This person may not talk at the beginning, and a leader cannot force one into it. An introvert may not be comfortable you put on the spot, so one must be patient and be smart enough to engage the team member, taking it slowly and gradually.

Find your own unique way of getting to know the team and rest assured that the process need not be formal. Agile is, in fact, definitely less formal and offers open policies to showcase those on your team from the first encounter. There is no requirement to wear a full suit when catching up with a test analyst for the first time. Most of the scrum masters I know are casual in terms of clothing; they may even wear jeans and t-shirts. Although this has not been proven through research, I found it is easier to strike up a normal conversation and to get to know one another when in casual wear.

Don't try to be formal and build gaps between you and your team members. I remember working in Singapore when I would often take my team members for a walk around Marina Bay. I noticed that the environment allowed them to be more relaxed and less formal.

Listen a lot.

I cannot stress this enough. When meeting team members for the first time, do not try to showcase your experience or knowledge.

Steer clear of mentioning accomplishments that make you proud when initiating conversations with the team. These sessions should be about them, not about you. Build an environment in which they can start talking about their own backgrounds, about their hobbies and their motivations and experience. That is how you convince them that you are there to listen to them, not the other way around.

Make your team

Once I was given a team of eighteen and asked to run the project in Agile, as the company wanted to introduce Agile organization-wide. I was puzzled about how to start an Agile (or Scrum) project with an 18-member team. I had a few options:

- Start the project with the team of eighteen and try to implement Agile.
- Challenge the team size and restructure the team.

I decided to choose option 2. I explained the principle of self-organized teams and why small team sizes are more effective. Management listened and agreed with some of the rationale, like difficulty in communication with larger team sizes. Finally, we created three small teams, each responsible for delivering one different feature of the same product, and the results were very pleasing. The point I want to highlight here is that **it is not necessary to blindly accept what is given**. As a scrum master, you know the Agile concepts, principles, best practices, and anti-Agile patterns, so you should show leadership and make the necessary changes when required.

Team size matters

Jeff Bezos, the founder of Amazon, introduced the **two-pizza rule** at the beginning days of Amazon. According to the rule, teams should be small enough to be fed with two pizzas. Although Bezos introduced this rule to manage meeting productivity, this rule is now widely used in Agile teams. Efficiency and scalability are the focus of this rule: what we see is that smaller sized teams bring a great amount of productivity by making face-to-face communications that help to remove delays in the value stream. So, whenever working with large teams, split them logically to create smaller teams.

Composition matters

In order to bring productivity, the composition of the team matters. Once I had a team of 80 percent UX designers and 20 percent software engineers working toward developing an ecommerce solution. Leadership had decided that user experience was one of the main things needed to crack, as this was a new initiative, so they hired as many user-experience designers as possible to join the team.

User experience designers took their role seriously and tried to propose the best user experience. Two software engineers were finding it very difficult because the UX designs proposed were not implementable or feasible due to technical difficulties. The UX designers did not understand that and they fought hard, trying to convince the software engineers that the designs were the best. The software engineers felt exhausted and expressed their wish to leave the team and join another team, or alternatively to even leave the organization.

Finally, during retrospective their sentiments came out and we agreed something needed to be done. We understood that the team was not balanced. As a result, we added one more software engineer, testers, and we also released three UX designers from the team. Finally it was a well-balanced team made up of two UX designers, two testers, three software engineers, and one business analyst. It did not take even one sprint to see some good results. The team bonded so well, and a workable solution was released within just two sprints. Just adding more and more resource persons is not a helpful unless it results in the right balance on the team. The moral of the story is that before really starting the project, analyze the skill set of the team and create the team accordingly.

Meet the product owner

The relationship you develop with the product owner is **paramount** to the success of your Agile project and of the team. If there is a good relationship with the product owner, it will make life and the project easier. Product owners need help from you in return, but some product owners may not know what help they need; that said, it is important to understand a product owner's background because through that you can determine where the best starting point is. For example, if the product owner has no experience with Agile, then he or she probably may not understand what you mean by a 'user story' or how to write one, let alone what pre-work needs to be done. But if the product owner has some experience, and if you start from the beginning and treat him or her with basic stuff, the product owner may get annoyed, considering how busy most people are. Think about the importance of getting this right, and right from the very beginning.

Chances are that your product owner is new to Agile, new to the product, has other BAU responsibilities, and has been asked to lead another product development as well. Most of the time (especially those who are new to Agile), this is the situation. Sometimes they have attended the Agile trainings, but it still would take some time to get into the Agile mindset. For example, they would not understand the concept of the pull system, and they will try to tell the team how many features they should develop—and how to develop them. So, getting him or her into the Agile mindset takes time, as well as tactful discussions and coaching. These kind of discussions with the product owner at the very beginning are vital. Assist him or her where help is needed. Work hard to understand what the person knows about the product, if there is a problem the product is required to solve, if there are any timelines that need to be adhered to, or any milestones or release deadlines. Find out if the product owner has identified the stakeholders, and if the answer to most of the above is negative, then it means you should hold a discovery session in order to come up with the product vision, roadmap, and backlog. However, since these are the responsibilities of the product owner, you can provide guidance to ensure the particular product owner meets with the stakeholders to have initial discussions and to understand any milestones required.

If the product owner is part of another BAU function and as such not dedicated to your project, then explain those commitments and spell out his or her responsibilities in terms of prioritizing product features, acceptance criteria, availability for the team, and any other important aspects. Consider even proposing to have that discussion with whoever appointed him or her to the project and announce that you can support him or her in developing a convincing case that proves helpful to the project. But, in the worst-case scenario where that proves impossible, understand where the product owner needs to be flexible – and conversely, where your team also needs to show flexible as well. For example, it is a must that the product owner attends the sprint planning session.

Understand the product owner's maturity level in terms of Agile. If he or she is not at all familiar with Agile, then recommend attendance at some product owner training. It is important that a product owner has the appropriate Agile mindset and understands what your team is talking about. I stress the **Agile mindset** because those who come from the traditional waterfall background, with a command and control mindset, tend to play the blame game when things go wrong. Such product owners will start building pressure on the team and blame the team for not achieving their commitments. This should not happen in an Agile project: winning or losing is a team commitment. The product owner and the scrum master represent the team. If you fail, you fail as a team, and as the product owner or scrum master, you bear the responsibility for the failure. On the flip side, if you are winning, the credit goes to the entire team as well.

The first meeting that needs to be held is to help build the relationship between you as the scrum master and the product owner. All of the items mentioned above are not going to happen during the first meeting. Subsequent sessions or coffee chats with the product owner may be required, and perhaps on a regular basis. But the first meeting should build the foundation for those. To understand his or her style of working and identify where you could be of help in the Agile journey, identify the friend within – and the befriend! Once you manage to do that you are going to have it easy, and your project is bound to be a success.

Meet other stakeholders

Your project may have many stakeholders, and it's typical for different stakeholders to bring different objectives. For example, a project manager of a project may be interested in delivering the project on time and within budget.

Apart from understanding the determined objectives, you may need to explain the project objectives, how you intend to work, what ceremonies there will be, and how the stakeholders should interact along the way. This is considering the stakeholder may not have any idea how you intend to go about the project operations.

In Agile, team members should be dedicated as opposed to being assigned to multiple projects. Your stakeholders may not know this, so they may try to assign team members to other projects that might end up causing conflicts. In such cases, you may need to talk to those managers and explain how context switching causes productivity loss. Explain the benefits of not assigning team members to multiple projects.

Explain cadence to your stake holders. Explain the scrum ceremonies involved and when they can join in. For example, a standup is not a session for all the managers to get status updates.

If they want status updates or if they questions, they should talk to you as the scrum master. Team members should not be disturbed. Let all the stakeholders know they are, though, welcome to attend the Sprint Review (showcase) as this is the time to engage team members and give product feedback to the team. This awareness is important as it ensures the team is fully supported while at the same time providing stakeholders the level of participation that they need.

Conduct an agile training

I cannot stress enough the importance of Agile training at the beginning of an Agile project, especially if the team and the stakeholders are new to Agile. If I look back at the Agile projects that have had phenomenal success, 80 percent of them started with some Agile training. This helps to put everyone on the same page, gain productivity from the very first sprint, and make considerable progress towards the end product.

As of now everyone seems to have some understanding of Agile, and in fact, many people would declare they know Agile. However, they may come from different Agile backgrounds, and as such it becomes important to validate their assumptions and bring everyone onto the same page. The best way to do this is by hosting an Agile training session.

If many of the stakeholders are experienced in Agile, then you can definitely do this training, but in the case that you are not qualified to conduct such a session, arrange for a trainer to do it. If your organization has an Agile community of practice, assign a trainer from there, otherwise just get a consultant to handle the training. There are many options available, but the requirement is simple.

This training does not need to be heavy or complicated. Simply make certain to cover the topics below:

- Agile mindset
- Agile manifesto

- Agile principles
- Scrum framework (or the selected framework)
- Practices you will be following like sprint planning, stand-ups, retrospectives, and backlog planning
- Roles
- Responsibilities for each role
- How Agile requirements are captured (user stories, acceptance criteria, definition of 'done')
- Self-organization and expectations
- How to carry out collaboration (face-to-face communication, peer programming, shadowing, etc.)
- Expectations from stakeholders
- Tools you are going to use like Kanban walls – encourage them to visit
- Metrics to be produced, etc.

You can include the stakeholders in the training as well to make the session as interactive as possible.

Define the cadence

Cadence is the rhythm of operation. What are the sustainable movement activities in terms of Agile events? What are the events and how often do they happen in the context of determining the cadence? We don't need the team to feel overwhelmed by meetings. In fact, they sustainable amounts of planning time, talking time, and execution time in order to be productive.

One, two, three, or four-week sprints?

Sprint duration needs to be sustainable. The team should not feel pressured by short period sprints, so deciding the sprint duration is a critical decision for any Agile project.

There are various things to consider when deciding the sprint duration. A sprint can be one week long, two weeks, three weeks, or even four weeks. Four-week sprints are rare, but we have seen teams opt for it. Two-weeks sprints seem to be the most common, although one-week and three-week sprints are also popular.

A one-week sprint is ideal for seasoned Agile teams who have previously practiced that duration, and projects that require experimentation and quick client feedback, such as research, are suitable to one- week sprints. We have also seen IT development projects sustain one-week sprints.

Teams who are just starting Agile may feel intimidated and overwhelmed with one-week sprints, and so it is not the best option for them. Also, with distributed agile teams, it may not be of much benefit to have one-week sprints as time zone differences do not allow enough time for execution.

Three-week sprints are ideal for teams who deal with a number of dependencies from other teams and need continuous, shippable products at the end of every sprint. This longer duration allows enough execution time for such teams to go through all the phases and meet quality criteria required in the final product. It is also suitable for distributed teams.

We have, however, observed that three-week sprints can be a little slow sometimes, and teams go into a kind of hibernation situation in the middle of the sprint. Four-week sprints suffer the same predicament.

From my personal experience, two-week sprints are common and the most successful of all sprint durations. It is a sprint that allows enough planning and execution time while catering to distributed teams in multiple time zones.

Things to consider when deciding cadence

When is the best day to start the sprint and when is the best day to finish?

One of the clients I engaged recently has a global policy of flexi Friday every other week. That means two Fridays a month the team does not work. In such cases, starting the sprint on Monday and finishing it on Friday does not work. These are vital things to consider when deciding the cadence.

For example, if Monday is a busy day with other organizational engagements, then Monday is not the best day to start a sprint. And if the product owner is not available when the sprint is starting, then it is not a suitable day to start the sprint as we need product owner during sprint planning. Below are the questions to ask before deciding the cadence:

- When is the best day to start the sprint?
- When is the best day to finish the sprint?
- How long should sprint planning take?
- How long should the showcase be?
- How long is the retrospective?
- When is the best time to have standups?
- When is the best day to have backlog refinement?

Below is a sample cadence for a team that operates on two-week sprints:

Time												
						DAY						
AM	Monday	Tuesday	Wednesday	Thursday	Friday	Monday	Tuesday	Wednesday	Thursday	Friday	Monday	Tuesday
9.30			standup	standup	standup	standup	standup	standup	standup	standup		
10-12		Sprint Planning										
PM												
2-3						Backlog planning					Showcase	
3.30 - 4.30											Retrospective	

Figure 26: Cadence of a two weeks sprint

Who should decide the cadence?

As to who should decide the cadence, the simple answer is 'the team. The cadence should work for the team, and so you need to ask these questions before you can decide on the cadence; plan to do so in consultation with the team. You, as the scrum master, can propose the initial cadence, but then you get to open the discussion to the team for any adjustments they think necessary.

For example, you may decide the standup time is 8 am, but for some members that may not work if they use public transport. Give them enough time to settle down in the office and be ready a bit later for the standup, like 9:15 am. This works better than imposing the cadence.

Flexibility

Once determined, do not change the cadence on your own as the scrum master. For example, if you find that a two-week sprint is ideal and optimal, do not change that. You will get an indication within the first few sprints whether or not the cadence is appropriate. For instance, if you have a one-week sprint, discuss during the retrospectives whether or not the flow is on target, and if the team agrees it does not feel right, then change it to two weeks. However, once that change is in effect, it should not be changed again. The set cadence needs to be consistent as frequent changes are unproductive. Still, it does not mean that if one day the team cannot, with good reason, meet at 9:15 am for the standup that you cannot change the standup to 2:00 pm. But it should not always fluctuate; once the team finds the optimal time, stick with it.

Define workplace arrangements

Agile is an environment where ample collaboration, discussion, and negotiations happen. Productivity is realized by the team through open, face-to-face discussion, so the working environment needs to be supportive of such discussions.

For example, there is no point of having cubicles surrounded by walls and then asking the occupants to work in the Agile way. We have not seen any positive changes with such environments.

By workplace arrangement I mean a number of things as listed below:

- Where are individual team members going to sit?
- Is there is a dedicated room or workplace for them?
- Do they have enough collaboration tools like white boards or writing walls?
- Do they have an adequate supply of stationary such as post-it notes, sharpies, flip charts, white boards, notebooks, projectors, Kanban walls, and printers?
- Do they have an adequate supply of snacks, food, and coffee?

If you were surprised with some of the items, like snacks and coffee, don't be. What you need to do is discuss with the team how you are going to find the budget for those. See if the project has room in its budget for such comforts, and if not, discuss the issue with management. This is a small investment but goes a long way into making the teams happy, so it's worth considering.

Why Workplace Environment is Important

The simple answer is productivity! Most of the teams with which I've worked claimed that their work is intense and having small bites like snacks keeps them energized all the time. Almost all Agile practices like standup meetings, sprint planning, and showcases are face-to-face activities. Practices like using a visual Kanban wall, estimations, and playing poker need space. Apart from that, our aim is to build high performing teams. One thing behind high performing teams is the personal bonding of the team members, which is supported by generally created co-locations. They should not be separated by the walls that make it difficult to interact.

The team members' efforts should go to doing the work and not in finding a meeting room or determining people's availability through meeting schedules. If all people are co-located, they can talk naturally at any time. Such arrangements naturally end up maximizing productivity.

What if the organization does not provide the right environment?

The reality is that not all organizations that promise cultural changes and support for new initiatives like Agile end up actively doing it. Not that they do not want to sometimes, it is just that such changes are new to them. They may not understand Agile and will hire scrum masters, provide triaging, and just assume magic will happen overnight. Do not be surprised or discouraged if you do not get the expected support from organizations.

Instead, be the change agent. Discuss and explain to management why it is important to provide the appropriate environment. It is possible they will understand the rationale and provide what you need.

Be the leader. That is the least you can do when you have challenges. If the things you require are not provided, then create them by yourself. Nobody is stopping you from creating a visual Kanban wall by putting some tapes and writing on a wall. Use whatever wall space you can find and build the desired you want with the support of the team members.

I was once working for a giant tech company and I was supposed to kick off one of their big Agile projects. That company was process-oriented, and autonomy was the least of their priorities. Still, they wanted to start Agile.

The room that was provided for my team of fifteen was littered with eight big tables, leaving hardly any space to move around. Space to collaborate was nil. I asked the officials to remove a few tables and create more space, and they told me they had raised purchase orders meant for the suppliers who were providing the facilities. They said it would take at least two weeks for the suppliers to come and remove the tables to create the space I required. I sighed and waited until seven at night, after everybody had gone home, and then worked with another team member to move four tables to the pantry area. As for the rest of the four tables, we created four teams around them and right there we had what we needed. We then cleaned the room and went home like nothing had happened.

The next morning each team member was excited about the seating arrangement and the space they all of a sudden had. The best part came later. One of the senior executives was passing by our room but a few seconds later he came back inside "Wow, this is really great." He was impressed with the way the team was working. Soon it became the trend on that floor, and I saw almost all the rooms remove excessive tables and chairs that accommodated their small groups.

The point is that even if it is not given, create it. Agile teams are supposed to be self-organized, so create your environment. Also, no one else would know what you want anyway, so take the initiative to create the environment you want and need.

Conduct a discovery session

One of the most important things to handle prior to any project is to figure out just why you are doing the project assigned to you. What is the problem being solved by this project? What value is this project meant to deliver? Most of the project teams complain that they do not know why they are doing what they are doing. Surprisingly, some of the leaders are also not clear why they are starting the project. A discovery session is handy for helping resolve such situations.

What is the problem you are solving?

You can find out the problem you are solving during a discovery session, with all the stakeholders present, or at least with your team members and the product owner. Try to understand this question: "What is the problem we have to solve as a team?" This helps define the main reason your team has been formed. If you can provide a solution to the customer's problem, then your team would be providing and delivering big value to the them.

Ultimately, it's vital to ask the power question: "**How might we…?**" For example, if the customer has a problem of dropping sales, ask the power question, "How might we help increase the sales?" Then, hold some brainstorming sessions with the team as well as with the product owner, customers, and end users on hand. You will pull many ideas from everyone in attendance, including your own team, which can then be discussed with the product owner.

Who are your customers and what do they need?

In the exercise of prioritizing and seeking the right solution, you may need to think about your customer. Who is the customer for the product you are developing? What does this customer really want? Keep in mind that different customers need different things. For example, when building an ecommerce solution, the customers would be impressed with a search functionality that would help them more quickly find products, but the store manager's preference would be a different feature.

It is possible to determine what a customer would like by considering different **personas**. Below is an example. Your team can create as many personas as possible by brainstorming.

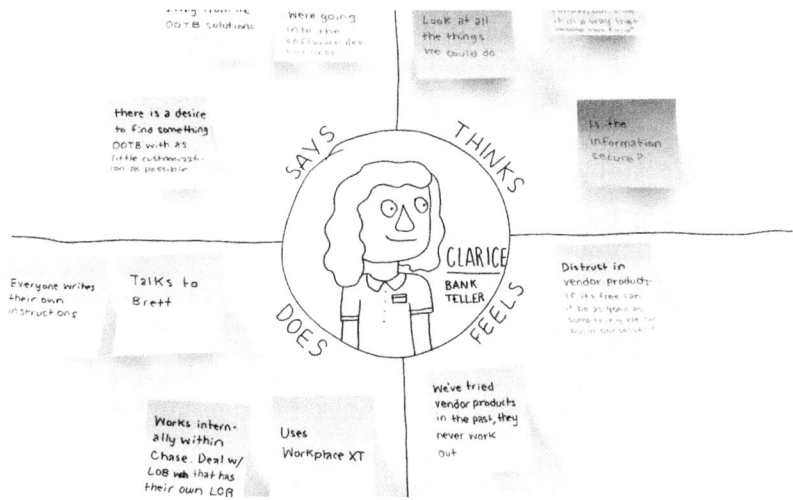

Figure 27: Persona (Image credit – IBM design thinking)

Check out IBM design thinking for more details on persona generation. https://www.slideshare.net/Dev_Events/ibm-design-thinking-the-bluemix-garage-method

Product vision

This is the section where you create a product vision based on issues or problems identified in the previous steps. If the product owner has these details in mind, then request that he or she explain it to the entire team. Otherwise, your team, along with the product owner, can create a product vision.

There are multiple ways to create a product vision, and below are two common formats:

Product vision template:

FOR < customer >

WHO < statement of the need>

THE <product name>

IS A <product category >

THAT < key benefits >

UNLIKE < competitors >

VALUE < further clarifications>

Let's simplify things by applying the format to this book as below.

FOR < aspiring new scrum masters >

WHO < needs to learn everything about becoming a Scrum Master>

THE <The Scrum Master>

IS A <book >

THAT < provides everything they need to know about a scrum master >

UNLIKE < other books >

This is a simple template which encourages both the team and product owner to think about all aspects of a product, especially factors such as competitive advantage and the unique values the product offers. The template helps the team to think differently and aim to deliver real value.

Another common use of templates is the business model canvas that is explained below.

Business modelling canvas

Business modelling canvas has proved popular among business owners and product managers. Although it looks like a product vision template, it also goes a little deeper in trying to dig for more details about the product.

Below is an example of the business modelling canvas applied to the LinkedIn business model.

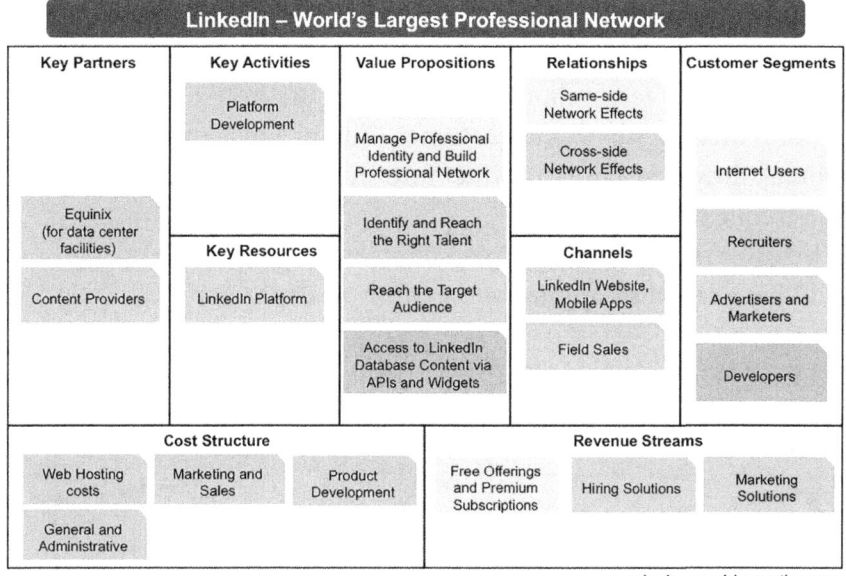

Figure 28: business model canvas (Thebusinessmodelgeneration.com)

It is up to the product owner to decide the level of detail required at this level; however, we have seen that a simple version of the product vision is sometimes more than enough to kickstart the project.

Product roadmap and backlog

According to Roman Pichler, "A product roadmap is a high-level, strategic plan which describes how the product is likely to develop and grow over the next months" (Pichler, R., http://www.romanpichler.com/blog/goal-oriented-agile-product-roadmap/). Roman Pichler is a well known product manager who tried to apply Agile principles in his product development. I have found his proposed methodologies helpful, especially when developing a product within an Agile environment.

Developing a product takes time, but this does not mean that a customer must wait forever to receive the product. If carefully planned, value can be delivered incrementally. As such, the product owner and the team should think about the best time to release product increments to the customer. The product road map helps to break down the entire product into smaller chunks and to deliver on a frequent basis.

Below is the product roadmap template Roman Pichler proposes, and I have seen this applied successfully in the real world.

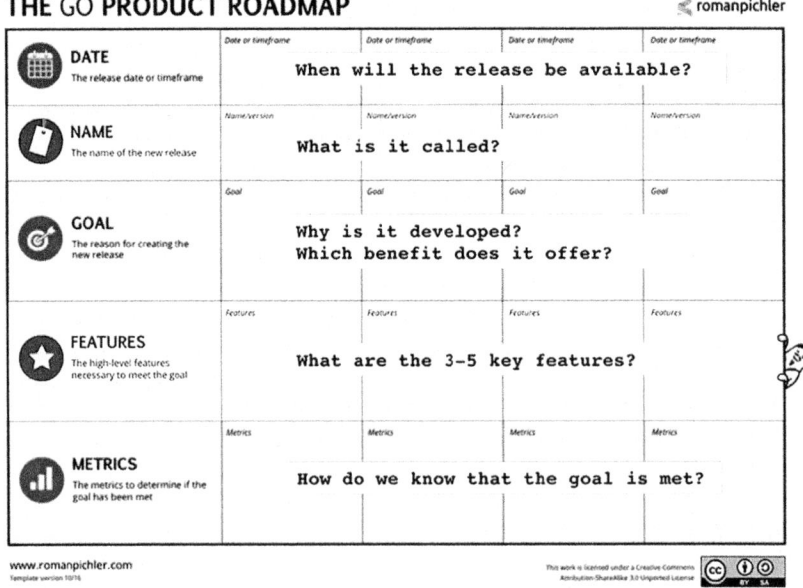

Figure 29: Product roadmap template (www.romanpichler.com, 2016)

Creating product backlog

As the above makes clear, the product roadmap template breaks down the entire product into features that deliver incremental value. The product owner and the team can further deconstruct these product features into user stories that ultimately create the product backlog for the team.

Those user stories can then be prioritized by the product owner based on aspects such as the roadmap and business value. At the end of this exercise, the team will have a prioritized product backlog, which is the final goal of the discovery session.

When the first sprint starts, the team should have a set of user stories from which to select for the first sprint scope. This discovery session will have helped the product owner as well as the team to create a starting product backlog.

Scrum Master's role in the discovery session

The scrum master plays a major role in the discovery session, including guiding the product owner in starting a discovery session and determining what needs to be achieved by the end of the discovery session. The scrum master mediates and facilitates the discovery session, but it is effectively led by the product owner and the team.

CHAPTER 9

Scrum Master's Responsibilities once the project has started

I N THIS CHAPTER, we will investigate the responsibilities of a scrum master as the project is executed. This is the phase where most of the activities happen. In this phase, the scrum master's fulltime dedication is critical.

The scrum master becomes instrumental in this phase, and often wears multiple hats. One must maintain a nice balance between being a coach and being a servant leader in order to help the team stay calm and focused during this phase.

Until the team becomes autonomous and self-organizing, which only happens over a period of time, there is significant involvement of the scrum master during the project execution phase. Depending on the maturity of Agile practices, the organization and PMO can also demand much from the scrum master as they require constant updates regarding the ongoing work. This is also where the product owner requires support to do his or her part in ensuring that the correct right process and practices are being followed during project execution.

It's obvious that as scrum master, one is intensely involved during this phase and as such, one needs to be properly prepared for it. Agile is an environment where things happen quickly, and high energy is essential. Otherwise, an extra dose of motivation and excitement during this phase will do the trick.

Below are a scrum master's responsibilities during this phase.

Be the servant leader

"Good leaders must first become good servants."

—Robert K. Greenleaf

Real Story

Jenny was a scrum master who emerged from a corporate background. She had been appointed as scrum master for a team of eight, within a financial institution that was very traditional. When the organization decided to move to Agile, Jenny was picked as scrum master for one of the teams. She felt privileged to be appointed to help in this transformation as part of the first wave leaders; still, she had the baggage of the hierarchical structure that she was, and remained, a part of.

The team she was leading owned one of the main strategic themes and it was very motivated. They were actually living and breathing Agile. However, it was not the same for Jenny. Due to the corporate culture, Jenny did not have a smooth ride. She was constantly bombarded with corporate meetings, ad hoc reporting, and presentations. Even though the team continued to use two-week sprints, Jenny felt like she was constantly under stress, and when this happened she became a different person altogether and forgot all the Agile values.

Once, during a rough sprint (due to unplanned work and last-minute bugs the team had found), the team decided to work nonstop to finish the work they had committed to. It was not a decision arrived at by management but by the team members themselves. They had decided they were going to finish the work and so they stayed late. They were very exhausted, but remained determined to finish the work, no matter how long it took.

It got to be about 6:30 pm, not the norm for this team that operated on a clear-cut rule of time boxing. In fact, by 5 pm, everyone was required to be out the office. But this particular day was different in regards to closing time. Jenny too stayed behind but she went to a corner somewhere isolated from the team and started working on a presentation. Realizing how exhausted the team was, the Agile coach reached out to Jenny and said,

"Well, they seem really stressed."

"Well, everyone is stressed, right?" she replied to the Agile coach.

"Is there anything you can do to ease the stress or to support them?"

"Nothing. What can I do? They found a bug. If they do a crappy job they should fix it," she replied.

"Well, they are doing it, aren't they? Actually, it is good as they are showcasing self-organization and autonomy. But, what can you do here?"

"Nothing," Jenny replied bluntly.

"What if you order them coffee or some snacks? I think they would appreciate it."

"What! You must be kidding, right? I am not a tea girl or a butler to serve coffee," the scrum master replied.

The scrum master is a servant leader. Research conducted by Holtzhausen and De Klerk concluded that there is a moderately storing correlation between a team's effectiveness and the servant

leadership of the scrum master. The research conducted involved 71 scrum team members and 22 scrum masters (Holtzhausen, & De Klerk, 2018).

Becoming a servant leader requires a shift of mindset. Making yourself available for the team is the beginning of that shift. You need to be approachable, easy to contact, and easy to talk to. During this phase the scrum master can become very busy, but that should not be a hindrance to the team. You should be mature and smart enough to manage your business and be available to the team. In short, the team must remain the number one priority.

Be the cheer leader

During the execution of the project, the team is going to fail certainly—and many times. This is understandable especially if the team is new to Agile and if the product is challenging. Below are a few things that can go wrong during the execution phase:

- Estimates can be wrong.
- Committed work during the sprint may not be achieved.
- The team may feel the pressure from the business.
- The team may receive negative feedback during the showcase.
- The team may witness conflict among themselves.
- The team may feel pressure from the product owner.
- The team may feel challenged by the Agile processes, such as transparency, stand-ups, and updating the Kanban wall.

This list can go on and on but the items above are the ones I have often seen in almost every project. This is the time one must be true and close to the team, like a good friend does, not abandoning the team at their most difficult times. The scrum master should constantly remind the team that it is all right to fail. In fact, Agile is a failure-friendly environment. We fail fast in Agile, but we also learn why we fail during the retrospective and take the actions necessary to learn from mistakes made. Do not judge the team or criticize them in a negative way just because they have failed during a given sprint. Instead, motivate them and point out to them the good things they have done as you help them bring out their best.

Remove impediments

Tim is a software engineer on the Avengers squad that is building an e-Commerce platform. The e-Commerce platform is one of the highest priorities for the company.

Avengers, who are a self-organized, autonomous team of eight brilliant people, are facilitated by Mark the scrum master and Jenny the product owner. They operate in two-week sprints and their focus in this sprint is to build the product catalogue and the home page. Tim owns the product catalogue and has made good progress.

Four days ahead of the sprint, Tim informed Mark that they need help. During the team standup, where the team met every day at 10:30 am, Tim announced that he has requested Jain the Marketing Manager to approve his catalogue contents, but that he had not heard from her three days. Tim tried contacting her a few times but received no positive feedback. With that, Tim cannot move forward with the rest of the development.

He had provided this update two days prior, and he promised to walk to Jain's office to discuss things; today he is reporting an update as, "Literally I cannot do anything now. I have tried everything. But I am stuck." Now he is looking at Mark, the scrum master.

If you were Mark, what would you do?

As a scrum master you will often be facing situations like the above. Below are a few complaints that you will hear from team members:

- I cannot finish the code review, as Mark is not available.

- The development environment is down, and we cannot get the latest code.

- The test environment is down and we cannot test.

- Arjun is sick and off for few days and as of now, I am dependent on his input.

- The product owner is unavailable, and I have this question. Without clarity, I cannot move forward.

- My computer is really slow, and I cannot really do any work.

- I don't have a head set and I cannot even join conference calls.

- We don't have any test devices. We need an iPad, galaxy tab, and windows tab to test the app. Our purchase orders have been rejected and we literally don't have any devices to test.

- None of the printers are working here and we cannot really test the print-out functionality.

Now, what is your role in solving these problems? I have heard some scrum masters say that the team should take ownership and solve the problems themselves. Yes, that is indeed the final goal. But it is a journey. Until they get there, it is scrum master's job to help to resolve these impediments. If the team needs help, then you as the scrum master should step in and help.

It is absolutely your responsibility to help the team resolve impediments. Below is a list of things you can try:

- **Stay calm and be patient**:

  It is possible that you can get overwhelmed by the number of impediments team members report or by the complexity and impact. You may not understand it first, and that is okay. You are not the person who has been doing that work so obviously you may not understand it. Do not get intimidated or stressed out from the magnitude of the impact. Stay calm.

- **Be empathetic**:

  Acknowledge and feel the frustration of the team members. Trust them when they say they tried. They would not be reporting negative results if they could successfully solve a pending problem. And their intention of reporting it is to find a solution sooner than later. Just be with them and understand.

- **Go for the coaching mode**:

  It is not expected that you alone solve all the problems. It is a team. Use the collaborative approach. Simply ask, "Ok, what can we do here?" Open a forum for collective thinking. You may be surprised that team members will come up with different options that you may not have even thought about. Some team members will offer to help, and below are some answers I have heard as resolution for the above question.

  - Okay, let me peer review on behalf of Arjun. Is that okay?
  - Let me test on behalf of you.
  - Okay, I know the marketing manager. Let me try to find what is happening there.

- Well, I know one of the team members in infrastructure. Shall I talk to him and see?

- I think we should set up a meeting with them and explain the urgency or go there and sit with them.

- **Gather information:**

  If the issue/impediment/risk is serious and you have to take help from external parties, gather information before reaching out external parties. It is likely necessary that you sit with the team member who has the issue to better understand the details. When the external party asks for more details, you must be able to at least articulate the issue and the impact. Hence, get more information and understand the issue or impediment in detail.

- **Use your network:**

  Sometimes it is just a matter of a phone call or just a coffee chat. What I have noticed in most of these cases is that the issue has not been discussed with the correct person, that is, the one who can solve it, like a supplier, vendor, or external team member. If it had been discussed directly with the appropriate contact, the issue could have been resolved on the spot.

  Another issue is that we depend on emails as the communication channel. We send message after message and the recipient replies with another email just asking for clarification on a question; then, the answer is given in another email, and then another email with another follow-up question, and the chain goes on. In between these emails, days can be lost. Had it been a face-to-face chat, questions, answers, and clarifications could have been offered on the spot, saving all those wasteful days. In such a case, you probably just need to meet the person and establish some relationship, and probably connect your team members by introducing them and giving them some authority to communicate directly.

- **Escalate if required**:

  Sometimes it is necessary to involve the people who have authority beyond your control to address certain issues. Consider your PMO, Product Manager, or senior leaders who may be able to help or at least direct you in the right direction. The moral of the story: seek help.

Manage conflicts

I have never seen a team where there are no any conflicts among team members. Coming from different industrial and cultural backgrounds, and then being charged with working together, a group will always encounter some conflicts. Healthy conflicts are good. But if things turn to the unhealthy and if the team is spoiled, the scrum master must intervene. As scrum master, one cannot turn a blind eye when friction among team members emerges.

Leo and Jenny both are user experience designers working in the Squad, workplace design. Both of them are highly talented, motivated, and passionate about the work they are doing. Their team is working in full Agile, and they are an autonomous, self-organized team.

In the middle of the fifth sprint (which means this team has worked together nearly three months), Leo approached the scrum master, Kate. "Can I talk to you in private, please?" he asked. "Sure," Kate replied and they walked out of the building into a closed meeting room.

"What's up, buddy?" asked Kate.

"I cannot work with Jenny anymore," Leo told her. Kate was surprised and saw tears bubbling up in Leo's eyes. So far, Kate had not heard any complaints from Leo, and in fact he had been supportive of other team members and had always maintained a positive vibe. He was the ice breaker on the team and now here he was, in tears, but struggling to hide his emotions. Once Kate said, "It's okay, Leo," he broke down.

"You know I like her. I do. She is really talented and to be frank, there is a lot for me to learn from her, but you know I am coming from a technical background too, so I want to let them know that some design decisions are not workable, technically. But she cuts me off all the time. She simply does not listen, so what is the point if I cannot air my views? And if she wants to implement only her ideas, why am I here? She just makes me feel like I don't know my job and that she somehow knows everything. I do like the rest of the team. They are really good but I cannot stand this anymore. If possible, I need to move to the other team. Can you please help me with that?"

★★★★★★★★★★★★

Developing a self-organized team is easier said than done. This kind of team is an organization in and of itself – just like a normal enterprise. When a small team works together for a longer period of time, there is one thing that is inevitable: conflict. I have never seen a team without conflicts.

How each team manages conflicts is individual and unique to the team. Up to a certain point, individual behaviors and personalities of team members come into the picture. Some team members opt to ignore the minor issues with their team members, but others may not.

Managing conflicts takes experience, and a scrum master is expected to come prepared. Below are few things to do:

- **Empathize and acknowledge feelings and emotions of individuals**: Don't say things like, "You are overreacting," or, "I am sure he did not mean it," or, "You need to be more open-minded." Likewise, never announce, "I am very busy" and then dismiss someone who needs your help.

- **Don't judge**: You really don't know what has happened, so don't jump quickly to conclusions. Even if you have one, keep it to yourself for the time being.

- **Be the coach**: After listening without any judgment and making sure that it is okay to talk about it, start a little bit of coaching and ask what else the person has to say about the situation.

- **Ask what the reporting person can do**: It's sometimes surprising that when asked this question right after unloading emotions, a team member may on his or her own come up with a good resolution. In the scenario above, Leo said, "I think I need to talk to her personally and see her side." This is really a smart answer and demonstrated that most of the time, the reporting employee may be able to come up with some answers on his or her own.

- **Offer some suggestions**: If the reporting team member can't come up with of reasonable solution, then as scrum master you can probably suggest something. Propose a talk with the other person where a heart-to-heart chat helps a team member explain how he or she feels.

- **Mediate the situation**: Although rare, sometimes the situation requires meditation. If all the previous steps fail, your involvement as a mediator is required. Facilitate a session between the two members. Most often you will just become the middle person, and they will start talking to each other. Do not jump in unless required. Listen. Let them talk to each other and hear the different sides. Stop offering solutions.

- **Come up with an action plan**: After understanding each other's sides, and with the agreement of each, come up with an action plan in which both members will take ownership. Discuss a good follow-up time to discuss the progress (e.g., after two weeks).

- **Give individual coaching**: While they are working on each other's actions, you can coach them individually. If uncomfortable or not skilled to do so, refer them to a coach or a mentor.

- **Take action if the situation is not improving:** It is rare that things go this far in conflict management, since most of the time team members will find their balance with a bit of coaching and mediation. But sometimes it just happens, and then action needs to be taken. These actions can be different from situation to situation. In the Leo and Jenny situation above, Kate had to talk to provide Jenny's reporting manager some feedback then ask him to coach her as it was the case that Jenny had been a bit difficult to Leo.

Do Coaching

As per Sir John Whitmore, "Coaching is focusing on future possibilities, not past mistakes" (Whitmore J. , 2017, pg 11). It is a relationship built between the coach and the coached. Once a project starts, as scrum master you must start this journey with all of your team members, product owners, and even with your stakeholders. Let's discuss these in detail.

Team coaching

Coaching is an essential skillset for a scrum master. The *Oxford Dictionary* defines a coach as "an instructor or trainer in sport," and "a private tutor who gives extra teaching." One of the best ways to explain this is by asking readers to watch a small clip from the movie *Chuck De India*. I am not a big movie fan (I simply don't have the patience to sit and watch a movie for two or more hours unless it is really, really good), but I would not mind watching *Chuck De India* again and again, even though I don't understand the language. This movie was a Bollywood super hit, not just because of the super star Sharukh Khan, but because the story line and the extraordinary performance by each crew member.

This movie clip explains the role of a coach very well.

https://www.youtube.com/watch?v=rrH90zd9uco

One of the jobs of a scrum master is to build a high-performance team.

A coach helps team to realize that the solution is within them. When one plays the role of coach, he or she purposely stays away from giving solutions. How to take team members on the journey to realize that the solutions are within them is a skill set one must develop.

Coaching product owner

Apart from coaching the team, you may have to coach your product owner as well. This may be especially true at the beginning of the project, and if the product owner is new to Agile practices, in which case the product owner may need guidance towards practices in terms of product ownership. It could very well be geared more about crafting the solution or about user requirements of the product and helping the product owner's mindset shift towards Agile.

Product owners may need guidance on issues ranging from user story writing to acceptance criteria, as well as the definition of done. If required, provide examples so she or he understands what needs to be captured. But you may have to coach the product owner for more broader scope. Those could include helping the product owner to understand the bigger picture, like what value this product is delivering, or what is the roadmap and how to come up with a roadmap. That means you need to be knowledge and able to coach product owner.

Coaching the enterprise / organization

Just because the team is full Agile and you have built a self-organized, autonomous team of which you can be proud, doesn't mean that your job is finished. Although your team is fully agile, your organization may not be. Leaders in the organization also should be able to understand this new way of working which your team is working in. to do that you as the scrum master may have to coach them too.

Example

I once worked as delivery manager. My entire project was operating in Agile and teams followed two-week sprints, fully autonomous and self-organized. One of the executives requested the delivery framework, release cycle, and some other information in a presentation format. The scrum master prepared a presentation and mentioned that teams were operating in "two-week sprints." The executive called me and asked, "What is a sprint?" He explained to me that he does not understand that jargon and was trying to understand.

We must realize that just because the team is Agile does not mean that everyone else in the organization will know what you do and how you do it. So, if you have built such a productive way of working, then it would prove worthwhile if you help the rest of the organization understand the way you work.

Case study

For instance, one of the not-for profit organizations I worked for had a major issue with the enterprise service management (ServiceNOW) project they were running. The project was terribly behind schedule and off in scope. PMO was under huge pressure to get the project back on track. Because project was delayed and running over budget and both the project manager and senior business analyst had left the project, unable to cope the pressure. I forgot to mention, that project was fully waterfall.

The PMO and CTO decided to hire someone with Agile experience, thinking that converting the project was the only way to rescue the situation. They hired a project manager and a scrum master who were extremely experienced in Agile projects, but there remained a problem.

PMO was running completely on waterfall. At every steering committee meeting, the PMO and the CTO would ask the scrum master and project manager to update the presentation format, for example by applying corporate branding guidelines, logos, and correcting color themes from indigo blue to navy blue. The project manager and scrum master were trying to bring the project back on track using the Agile framework, and they were finding some success, but senior stakeholders like PMO, CTO, and CEO were thinking only about the presentation's visual appearance. Scrum master was frustrated.

Finally, the scrum master took a brave step to explain to the steering committee how Agile works. He explained the Agile manifesto as, "Working software over comprehensive documentation." He asserted that if they needed the project back on track, then the leadership team needed to stop asking for lower priority cosmetic changes and instead help in the areas identified by the project team. I was part of that meeting and I saw how the CEO listened then quickly assured the scrum master that they would be focusing on helping.

Having the scrum master play the role of change agent is important for the rest of the organization, as he or she can influence other stakeholders, especially those who are directly associated with the team and with the product. Inviting them for showcases, bringing them in for brown bag sessions about how the team operates, and allowing them to observe the workplace are impactful things you might do.

Enforcing Cadence

As human beings we are used to certain habits. Once the habits are built in our system, it is difficult to rid ourselves of them, even if there is a will to do so. It is equally as difficult to cultivate new habits, mostly because it's possible that we just revert to old habits instead.

Cadence is the rhythm in which Agile events happen. Cadence determines when events like sprint planning, stand-ups, backlog planning (or grooming), scrum of scrums, sprint showcase, and retrospectives (or sprint reviews) happens. The Agile team, product owner, and scrum master will define the cadence, when things need to happen, where, and for how long. Below is an example of such a cadence.

Event	Objective	Frequency	Duration	Participants
Sprint planning	• Define sprint goal • Define the sprint scope • Commit to sprint scope	Once in every sprint	Four hours (for two weeks sprint)	Product owner, scrum master, development team

Event	Objective	Frequency	Duration	Participants
Backlog refinement (grooming)	• Refine the backlog and make it up-to-date • Prioritize user stories based on the business requirements or changes • Add enough details to the user stories	Once a week	Two hours (depends on the sprint duration, two hours for two weeks sprint, but should be decided by product owner and the team)	Product owner, Development Team Scrum Master Main stakeholders if possible
Sprint Showcase	• Show-case the product features which have been developed in the sprint • Take customer feedback	Once in every sprint	At least two hours (but should be customized depending on the number of stakeholders and numbers of features)	All stakeholders, customers, entire development team, product owner, scrum master

Event	Objective	Frequency	Duration	Participants
Sprint Retrospective	• Identify what worked well and why • What improvements are required and committing to improve those	Once in every sprint (at the end of the sprint)	At least one hour (should be customized based on the activity of the team)	Entire team
Daily standup	• Updating the entire team on the progress made towards achieving sprint goals • Updating the entire team on what slow them down and take actions	Every day	Fifteen minutes (for a scrum team of 7 to 9)	Entire team including product owner

Event	Objective	Frequency	Duration	Participants
Scrum of scrum	• Updating each scrum team on the progress made by each team • Get help from each other team if required	At least twice a week (depending on the number of squads, urgency or the product etc. should be customized based on the product and releases)	At least half an hour	All scrum masters of each squad or a designated team member

But following this cadence is difficult at the beginning of any Agile team. People don't show up on time for stand-ups, backlog planning is skipped, or retrospectives are de-prioritized. Still, Agile teams cannot afford to cultivate these anti-patterns and not take any action. As scrum master, it will be your job to enforce the cadence and cultivate these new habits.

I remember one of the team members on one Agile team who normally did not come to the standup meeting. The rest of the members did come and gave their updates, but this guy liked to work behind his computer. When I asked why he missed these meetings, he said, "I do work. I finish my work. When I finish my work, I do email the project manager giving the update. Why do I have to talk about it in front of everyone? Nobody asked me to do that before." For most of the people who are new to Agile, it is difficult to break from the old mindset of 'me and my work.'

So, when you manage to get the team to follow the cadence, to understand individual concerns and the justifications they have in their own minds. Then, address these accordingly because unless you find the root cause, things will not change.

You must be tactful when trying to get the cadence up and running. Whether you have to bring food to each and every meeting, gamify it, block in the calendars, walk to each of them and ask for them to join the meetings and follow the cadence is dependent on the situation and on the maturity of the team. However, doing it is absolutely necessary at the beginning of the project until the team absorbs the rhythm.

Facilitate Scrum events

During the project execution, your team is going to have many events which we normally call Agile ceremonies; some will to the team and some will be external. Most of these events need to be led by the scrum master. Their ceremonies may be different from framework to framework.

Let's discuss in detail what to do—and how and when to do it—when facilitating these events.

1 Sprint Planning

As most would agree, sprint planning is an essential and critical event of any Agile team. Sprint durations are fixed (one, two, three, or four weeks), and during the sprint planning a team decides what they are going to develop (scope), how to develop it, and how many they can develop. It is commitment between the product owner and the development team for the sprint duration.

During the sprint planning, a team needs to achieve the things listed below:

- Define sprint goal (i.e., home page of an ecommerce web site or chat box for a customer support function)
- Prioritize a list of product features for achieving the sprint goal (i.e., a chat box)
- Identify the user stories required as per product features and the sprint goal.
- Gain a clear understanding of the complexities and interdependencies, as well as a high-level plan of how they might be solved (not solutions)
- Identify what is committable and what is not committable as per the team velocity
- Secure that agreement between product owner and the team
- Commit the sprint scope

Below is a guide for use in successfully facilitating this event:

- Arrange a work area which facilitates open discussion and collaboration. If there is a dedicated war room with a Kanban wall, that would be best. Otherwise, get a room that is free from disturbances and one that allows collaboration, complete with writing boards and post-it notes.
- Prepare an agenda and confirm that the entire team and the product owner understand it. This is a time boxed event, so the outcome needs to be archived within the time frame allotted.

The agenda can look like the example below (modify as per your sprint planning session duration and other requirements):

- Announce the sprint goal – Product owner
- Provide the list of prioritized features and reasons behind the prioritization – Product owner

- Provide a list of high-level user stories – Product owner
- Discuss the user stories – Team
- Clarify the acceptance criteria – Product owner
- Declare the user story estimation – Team
- Select the user stories for the sprint – Team and product owner
- Commit the sprint scope – Product owner and team
- Arrange the Kanban wall or digital tool – Team

- Time box the event. Make sure that enough time is allotted and that the team is guided towards the completion of all items within the event's timeframe.

- Make sure everyone participates in the discussion, especially those team members who are shy or not actively participating. Engage your coaching skills to draw in those members who are not so keen on taking part.

- Facilitate the user story estimation. If your team is measuring the user stories using planning poker, then you can facilitate it by leading the planning poker session. You are not supposed to estimate the user stories or influence the estimates by any means. They are the people who will be doing the work so what matters is what they understand how complicated it is to the team.

- Make sure the team is challenged to gain clarity on the user stories, especially on acceptance criteria and on the definition of done (remind them if this been missed).

- Remember to finish the sprint planning session with a high motivational note. Remind them that they are a fantastic team and if they work collaboratively, they can chive the commitments.

2 Backlog Refinement (Grooming)

Backlog refinement/grooming is the activity which needs to happen to ensure that product priorities are updated with enough details, so that it is ready for the next sprint. Constant prioritization of the backlog is critical to value delivery by the team as priorities may have changed due to various reasons such as those listed below:

- Product owner have found more details on the high-level features previously identified.

- Customer feedback has been received on the previously released feature and some modifications are in order.

- High priority bugs have been identified and need modifications to the identified user stories.

- Dependencies have been identified which can impact existing priorities.

- Business priorities and strategies have changed, which in turn changes existing priorities.

- The product owner has submitted more detail relevant to the acceptance criteria of the existing user stories.

Considering the fact that Agile is fast paced and business requirements are changing constantly, backlog refinement at regular intervals is **essential** to maintaining the team's productivity. I have seen the clear difference between teams who do backlog refinement at regular intervals and the team who does not. Productivity and the value delivery of the teams who do backlog refinement is high compared to those who do not conduct it at regular intervals.

There is a tendency to skip this event. This is an anti-pattern. In such situations, the scrum master needs to coach the product owner to understand the difference between doing backlog refinement and not doing it.

Product owner's responsibility in backlog refinement

Backlog refinement needs pre-work by the product owner. In order to identify whether the business priorities have changed, the product owner must contact the business leaders and gather feedback. Acceptance criteria should have been identified and details should be made ready prior to the backlog refinement sessions. Otherwise, the session will be a waste and the team will not be prepared to help.

Scrum Master's Responsibility

Guide the product owner and the team to achieve the cited outcomes of the backlog planning session. Product features need be prioritized, those features need to be broken down to user stories, and necessary details should be added. Then, the user stories, which would be highly applicable to the next sprint, can be marked by the product owner.

Encourage and engage the team in the backlog refinement. It needs to be a collaborative session between the product owner and team. The team can contribute to refining technical or non-functional and quality details. As an example, priorities among things like performance, continuous integration, and reducing technical debts can be planned and discussed with the product owner.

Make sure the session is happening at regular intervals as per the cadence. What we have seen is that there is a tendency, by the product owner, to skip this session, especially if the product owner is allocated with other business-as-usual work. That is where the scrum master needs to guide and coach the product owner.

3 Daily Standup

Standup is one of the most important practices in a scrum team. Teams catch-up for fifteen minutes every day to update one another on the progress of the user stories worked out the day before. It sounds simple, but in action it can be difficult to have a successful standup. Below are the qualities of a **successful daily standup**:

- It is time boxed to exactly fifteen minutes.
- Each team member summarizes his or her update to fit the format and to give an update to all of the team members.
- The rest of the team members gain understanding about what each other is working on.
- Each team member understands what slows them down and takes immediate action to mitigate or solve issues.
- Each member asks for or offers help during the standup.
- Team members start the standup voluntarily, whether the scrum master is present or not.

It sounds like a simple agenda to meet, but the reality can be different, especially at the start of a project. And, the complexity would be much more intense if the team were new to Agile.

Difficulties of running a good standup

First, people fail to show up on time, and when they do show up, their updates may be too lengthy, causing the standup to run over the planned fifteen minutes. Moreover, updates may not be relevant to the tasks on which they worked. They may fail to report the problems and impediments encountered. Some team members are allowed to work from home so they may not attend the standup. Some team members will give very brief updates which do not make any sense, while some team members use mobile phones or laptops during the standup so that their full attention is not on the task at hand. Some members want to leave after giving their updates as they are busy, while the product owner may not even attend at all. Standups will not be conducted if the scrum master is absent, as some team members declare it a waste of time. People outside the team also may try to attend, which makes the standup longer.

This list can go on and on, making clear just how difficult it is to run a successful standup.

Guidelines

Below are a few guidelines to consider, but remember one must find unique solutions, dependent on each situation. In difficult circumstances, seek help from an Agile coach.

- **People don't show up for the standup**:

    There can be many reasons for this to happen. Below are few things you can check:

    - Is it scheduled for an appropriate time? As an example, 8:30 am can prove too early as people may be late thanks to a troublesome commute. Give them enough time to arrive, get coffee, and settle in. Check with the team about the ideal time to have the standup and then schedule accordingly.

    - At the very beginning of a project, the team may be unfamiliar with just what to do. Give a hint like, "It's standup time, guys," which will then become common practice.

    - After a few sprints, stop doing that and then congratulate those who came to the standup without any hints or reminders.

- **The standup exceeds 15 minutes**:
    - Guide those involved to prepare for the standup update prior to the event.

- Ask everyone to frame their updates in the format of "What I did yesterday, what I am doing today, and my blockers are…."
- If the update needs more details beyond the above format, ask them to take it off line.
- If more discussion is needed, ask them to stay after the standup with only those required to discuss the issue in more detail.
- Finish the standup within exactly fifteen minutes and leave the room.

- **The product owner fails to attend the standup:**
  - Have a chat with the product owner, one-on-one, to understand the rationale behind why he or she does not attend the standups.
  - Explain why it is important to attend the standups as their presence will help the team to make some decisions. Moreover, if the product owner attends the standup, it can expedite value delivery.

- **Impediments and problems are not raised at the standup:**
  - If team members are avoiding the impediments (which is possible at the beginning of a project), ask specific questions about impediments like, "What about the problems? Are you facing any or anticipating any issues?"
  - Help them to discover impediments early. For example, if a team member works on a user story and gives the same updates for three days continuously, ask questions like, "Do you have any dependencies?"

- **The standup is cancelled if the scrum master is absent:**
  - At the beginning of a project, the team may think that a standup should be conducted by the scrum master, so

if the scrum master is not there, they will not conduct one.

□   Explain that the standup needs to be conducted by the team, for the team. It is not for the scrum master. It is in fact their responsibility to get an update on each other's work in order to move forward as a team; whether or not the scrum master is present, it should happen. Congratulate the team that does carry through on a standup, even without a scrum master, so that such good behavior is encouraged.

One different challenge you may have to address is that some teams like to replace face-to-face standups with other channels like whatsapp group chats, standup chat bots, or other extensions of the latest technology. There is no harm of experimentation, however, as of now research has proven that face-to-face communication is the best when the goal is to improve collaboration and productivity by reducing waste.

4 Showcase/Sprint Review

Showcase or sprint review is the way to get regular customer feedback at the end of every sprint. This is one practice that aligns with the Agile principle of 'customer collaboration.'

Showcases are required and address many practical issues we have in the business world.

- Customers do not directly engage with the product, so they have no idea what the product looks like.
- Stakeholders who are contributing to the product also have no idea because they don't directly interact with the project team.
- End-users who are going to use the product have no idea how the product is working.

- End users/stakeholders have questions on why and how certain product features are prioritized over other desired features, so they would like to get some rationalization.

Showcase thus plays a huge role in addressing such issues. When an Agile project starts, this may be new to the team, as well as to your customers and stakeholders. Some extra effort will go a long way in building awareness. Note that the event is required at the very start of a project, as this is where awareness and vital guidance is required the most.

Some guidelines

Showcase plays a key role in building awareness. You must make sure it is added to the schedule in advance and explain the advantages of the showcase. As the scrum master, you must facilitate the session, but the product owner and the team need to run the show. They are the key players, after all.

Imagine this as a product road show. It is an interactive session, where your team explains the product and gives an opportunity to try it out, but they still need guidance about how to fit tasks to the sprint objective. That's where your direction comes in.

Achieving the objective of the showcase is important, so an agenda set up at the beginning is really helpful. In that way, you can frame the show around what your team has crafted. Below is a sample agenda, but feel free to customize as you see fit to suit your product or project, as well as the duration of the showcase.

Agenda item	Duration	Who owns it (name of the person)
Welcome the audience Kick off the showcase Set ground rules and explain the agenda	5 minutes	Scrum Master
Sprint goals	5 minutes	Product owner
Developed product feature 1	10 minutes	Team member 1
Questions and answers	5 minutes	Audience
Developed product feature 2	10 minutes	Team member 2
Questions and answers	5 minutes	Audience
Developed product feature 3	10 minutes	Team member 3
Questions and answers	5 minutes	Audience
Audience feedback	5 minutes	Audience

(Team member 1,2 and 3 above are those who contributed and own the development of the user story)

Your job here is to guide the audience, as well as your team, to stay on the topic. It is possible that the audience (stakeholders, customers) ask various questions from the development team and those inquiries may not align with the current sprint. Your team members or the product owner will try to answer those questions but by doing so, you will be losing the time to showcase what you have developed, which is the main point. Thus, you need to guard the agenda.

Below are few guidelines for facilitation of the showcase:

- **Set the expectation with your team to prepare for the showcase:**

  It should not be a surprise to your team; in other words, they should not be hearing about the showcase just one day prior to its execution. Preparation for the showcase should be one of their tasks in the sprint. In fact, in one my projects we added that as part of the 'definition of done' to the user story.

- **Book your audience well in advance:**

  Customers and stakeholders are very busy people. If you want their participation, book them in advance. Sending last-minute calendar invitations will not yield a positive outcome.

- **Set the agenda:**

  Managing the time is critical during the showcase. Your audience can be guided on what the team is going to showcase so they can frame their expectations around that very agenda. This will help present an organized, guided showcase rather than the team missing a good opportunity due to derailments.

- **Inform everyone about the ground rules**:

  This is one of the key elements of a successful showcase. The audience can include a mix of people with a variety of intentions. There will be people who support the product, those who do not like it, and people who were threatened by the product the team develops; there may even be people who try to showcase their own brilliance in the middle of a crowd. Since there is only a limited amount of time, plan to manage this time wisely to fulfil the objectives of the showcase, which is to showcase the product features and collect valuable feedback.

  Ground rules will set expectations and provide the framework to help keep things in focus. Include some of the parameters suggested below as ground rules:

  - No mobile phones or laptops.

  - Questions should relevant to the product features showcased.

  - If the answer takes more than ten minutes, then the team members will reach out to the questioner individually and respond after the showcase.

  - The session will be recorded for the benefit of those who could not attend.

- **Make sure each team member participates**:

  Your team has completed a list of product features. Each of them must have taken the lead or somehow own those features. So when presenting those features, ask them to lead. After all, they know the feature they developed so they are the best people for the job of presenting. Give them the honor and let them be heroes in front of their customers and stakeholders.

If, though, the situation is becoming tough as customers express negative feedback or if a team member is getting uncomfortable, save him or her. Interfere and navigate smartly and do not let a team member feel badly. In the end, it is teamwork, but being a good leader means you must step up when a team member is in trouble.

- **Make it interactive**:

  When applicable, let the audience use the features your team has developed. The showcase does not need to be based on presentations. Make it interactive when possible. For example, if presenting a mobile app, ask attendees to download the app on the spot and start using it. If you have a restriction on devices or if it's taking time to download, give out a few phones on which you've already set up the app. This makes it possible to capture the real-time feedback, like usability. Beyond that, things are more interesting in this case compared to another boring presentation.

- **Respect the audience and their feedback**:

  The audience is not predictable. They may like the product, team developed or not. But the team will always expect a positive outcome. They will imagine that the feature they developed will be well received and that the customer will be thrilled. If that happens, it is great.

  But if it does not happen, the team should take the negative feedback in a positive way. At the end of the day it is your customer and they are having trouble accepting the feature the team has built. If you are selling the product to them, it's possible they won't be buying anything if they see problems, so you have to welcome all sorts for feedback with an open mind and respect the customers' opinions.

- **Follow up with both attendees and non-attendees:**

  Once the showcase is finished, follow up with the audience by thanking them for attending the session and for giving feedback. Provide a summary with what data the team has captured. If there were any decisions made, like a feature is now accepted and ready for release, formalize that by providing the update for those who could not attend. A summary page is a good way to provide such updates.

  If you promised to reach out with further details, make sure you or the team members do indeed reach out on time. They have asked questions because they were interested in your product, so follow up with them after the session.

5 Sprint Retrospective/Review

Agile takes continuous improvement seriously. No process can be optimized if it is not improved on a regular basis. Agile teams review their process at regular intervals (i.e., in every sprint), so these reviews, normally referred to as retrospectives, are critical and should happen at the end of every sprint.

Teams look back on the process they follow to determine what worked for them and what did not. If something has worked, then they can make a decision to continue it in the next sprint, but if it hasn't then they can discuss why it failed. This is normally the nature of a sprint retrospective.

To gain all the benefits of Agile teams, you as scrum master must make certain that the below tasks are done during the retrospectives:

- **Conduct the retrospectives at regular intervals:**

  Retrospectives must be conducted at the end of every sprint. These are **optional**. The sprint is an activity packed event and there are many things that do work and many that do not. If something is not working, there is no point in continuing it in the next sprint. This needs to be decided on quickly and on a regular basis, so again—the retrospective at the end of every sprint is essential to success.

One common pattern we identify from high performing scrum teams is that they never skip retrospectives. It is a scrum master's job to convince the team of this and to make retrospectives happen. Teams who are new to Agile or those with no agile expertise tend to skip retrospectives; in such a situation, work to persuade them to continue having sprint retrospectives.

- **Create a safe and trusted environment**:

  The retrospective is the team's event. Team members should be able to speak in a trusted environment. Team members should be able to critize their process and behaviors with trust and it should not be judged. Then only they will be honest in giving their feedback to make the process better.

  Sometimes senior managers including PMOs try to attend the session (I have witnessed a scrum master inviting the general manager to a retrospective), and scrum masters should take the lead to stop that. But make sure when you say, "No" to go on and explain to them why a manager's attendance may negatively impact the retrospective. Frankly, when managers are present, team members will not talk openly. They will always be conscious that they will be judged. Team members should not have that fear so limit attendance to the development team, product owner, and scrum master.

- **Make sure all the team members are active and participating**:

  Everyone's opinions and ideas matter. Sometimes it is possible that some team members may be silent during the retrospective, especially when discussing what needs to be improved. The scrum master needs to make sure that all team members are presenting their ideas for discussion. One way to do this is by using post-it notes. What I have noticed is that some people are comfortable writing down their thoughts, but they don't utter a word when asked to speak up. Figure out what works for your team and change the techniques in use accordingly.

- **Change the retrospectives formats based on the maturity of the team**:

  One complaint we get from teams are that retrospectives are wasteful events. At the beginning of the project they are normally very enthusiastic and engaged, but over time they find that retrospectives are boring and that no real improvements are happing.

In a way this is true. At every sprint you asked what worked well and what did not and how to improve. They identified a list of actions. And when it is done at the next sprint, it is the same process and the same actions. But there is no improvement and they go through the same set of issues at every sprint. This is indeed boring.

Consider addressing two things here:

1. Avoid monotony.
2. Make the actions work.

I will explain both in a sub-section below.

Avoid monotony

Add variations and diversity to retrospectives. This is the easiest way to break up the monotony. Following some of the guidance below and work on inventing your own methods.

- **Change the location of the retrospective:**

  Conduct the retrospective at different venues. It does not need to be in the everyday office work environment. Go to a park, a balcony, or an outdoor space if your company has one. Do it over a barbecue (before everyone gets drunk) or on a yacht. There are no limitations. Just make sure that you can still conduct a guided discussion, such as putting up a flip chart and asking the team to write on post-it notes and then discuss things without interruption.

- **Tell a story and use analogies:**

  There is no requirement to repeat the same story every time. You can add variations and even create your own formats. For example, below are a few common formats available to conduct retrospectives:

  - Traditional format
  - Sailing boat
  - Tree of us

  I would recommend you read the book *Retrospectives*. It explains more than fifty different types of retrospective formats which can be applied depending on the maturity of the team.

- **Bring a different facilitator:**

  There is no requirement that the session is only facilitated by you. If you have a good storyteller on your team, leverage him or her to facilitate the session. Use the skill set available in your team to get more variations.

  Bring in a scrum master or Agile coach from a different team. This is a very good way to add a bit of spice to the retro. Different people have different storytelling techniques, so just give your team a different flavor by bringing in someone from your outer circle.

Commit the actions

During the session, team members will identify and propose many actions that need to be executed in order to achieve expected improvements. However, the issue most of the time is that these actions are not executed by team members. During the sprint, product user stories will take the priority than the actions identified in the retrospective, so those improvement stories or actions will never be implemented. As scrum master, make sure that these actions taken by your team are getting priority and implementation.

Below is some guidance for achieving this with the team:

- **Prioritize the tasks identified during the retrospective and select only the top three to implement**:

    It will not be practical to select every action the team proposes. Identify the top prioritized actions.

    Ask who can take ownership of implementing those actions: Ownership does not mean the activity execution is his or her job, but it means that it is that designated person's accountability to make sure that rest of the team members are doing whatever they are supposed to do to implement the proposal.

- **Add the task to the visual Kanban wall and track it like a normal user story**: That means its update should be given at standup.

- **Add the results to the showcase**:

    If the team has managed significant improvement to how they operate, showcase that. It will be a good learning opportunity and useful knowledge sharing for stakeholders and customers alike, while demonstrating results of the continuous improvement.

6 Updating metrics

"Working software is the primary measure of progresses."(Scaled Agile Framework, 2018)

"Metrics. Do we need those? Aren't we supposed to produce working software? Isn't working software the final measurement, and if so, why do we have to have so many metrics?"

When I was a scrum master early in my Agile carrier, those were the questions I used to always ask, and I am certain you must be asking those questions as well.

Why are metrics important?

When I was studying at Oxford, we had an interesting subject—"Financial Management." Initially we all thought it was all about forecasting, creating budgets, and controlling it. But our perspectives were changed by Professor Paolo Quattrone who introduced us to 'maeauticmachines.'

One of the interesting things we learned was the purpose of metrics and of reports and discussions. "Project reports which showcase project metrics should ultimately encourage people/stakeholders to ask questions. When it does that, it brings people to seek help, find measures to make it right" (Paolo Quattrone, 2018).

That is why the metrics are required. They encourage us to ask questions and seek help in advance—before it is too late.

Right balance

We must, though, make sure to find the right balance. At the end of day, the only right measure is the working software/product. If there is no working product, there is no point of having many matrices. So, our metrics need to reflect the workability and usability of the product and show how far we are from making the product workable or consumable.

Below are a few metrics you can produce to reflect the above:

Burn down charts:

Burn down charts is the most common type of metrics at team level. When you are talking to project managers or stakeholders, they will at the very least be expecting this metrics so it makes sense to have it.

A burn down chart represents the amount of work done over time. You can capture this by calculating the total number of story points the team committed within the sprint and track how they were completed. Ideally at the end of the sprint it should become zero.

Below is a simplest sample burn down chart:

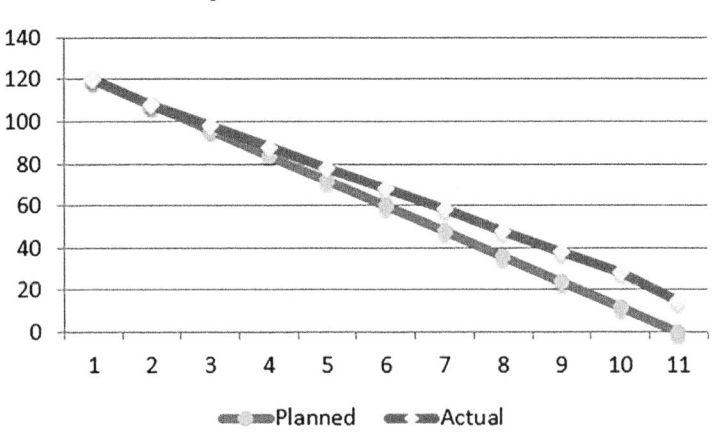

Chart 1: Burn down chart (Scaledagile.com)

The X axis represents the number of days in the sprint.

The Y axis represents the total story points of all the user stories in the sprint.

The blue line represents the ideal burn down.

The red line represents the burn down of each day.

Release burn down chart

In the sprint burn down chart you can get a sense of how your team is moving forward towards the various commitments of the sprint.

In a release burn down chart, we get a sense how the team is moving forward towards the commitment of a release. For example, your team may have decided that a few features are combined and then release them to the market for use by the customer. These product features were developed over a period of four sprints. In order to achieve this commitment, in each sprint your team must complete the commitments. The release burn down chart helps get a sense about this commitment to the release.

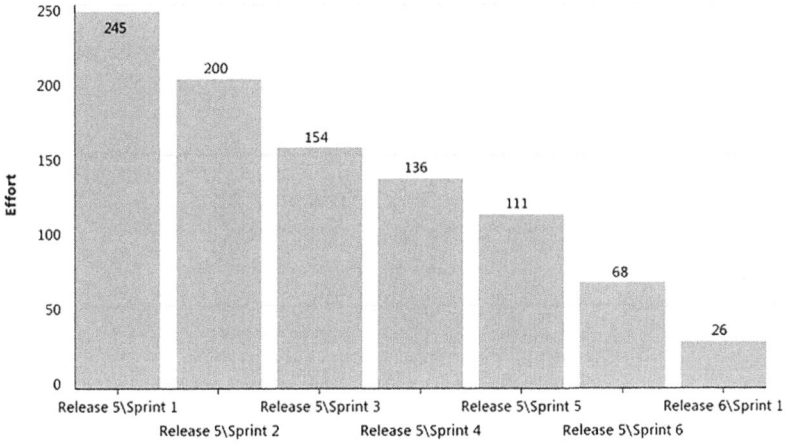

Chart 2: Release burn down chart

The X axis represents the sprint number.

The Y axis represents the total story points of all the user stories in the release.

Each bar repents how many story points were completed in each sprint.

Team velocity

Velocity is one metric which can be used to recognize how the team is improving in the process. It should be understood thoroughly. It is like a speed of a car: speed can be increased, but over a period of time it does not need to be faster and faster. What is required is that the team finds the optimal sustainable speed or velocity for the specific case.

Some teams put unnecessary focus on velocity. Some managers expect that in one sprint if the velocity is 100 story points, then the next one should be 150, and the next 200. However, it does not work like that. It is the scrum master's job to explain the concept of velocity to the team as well as other stakeholders. Otherwise stakeholders will be constantly asking the team and the scrum master to increase the velocity again and again.

In my viewpoint velocity should be used only to showcase that it will take few sprints to find the optimal velocity.

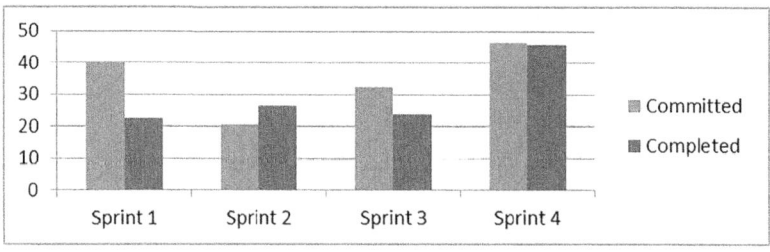

Chart 3 : Team velocity over a period of time

There are many metrics that you can produce but as mentioned, you need to find the fine balance here. At the same time, managers may be asking you to produce reports and metrics and you may be wondering the purpose of those reports. Then, in every sprint do a retrospective of each report as well.

- What was the purpose of the report?
- How many people have used that report?

- What purpose has it been used for?
- Is it worth producing these reports? If so, why?

You along with your managers and leaders should be continually asking these questions. If no significant value is perceived, then you should stop producing the reports, as there is no point producing waste. You should instead invest that time in supporting the team toward removing impediments or toward getting self-organized.

7 Scrum of Scrum

Developing a product or service requires the effort of multiple teams, just like an organization with multiple functions working together to build the company. The human resources department, finance department, operations, legal, supply chain, sales and marketing, and information technology are the sub teams who specialize in a specific function. Each provides a unique service to the entire organization, as well as to the other teams. But productivity is elevated when all teams synchronize as one. This is significant and critical if a product has services added by each team to make the full product. We call this a value stream.

Your scrum team is just one team in the value stream. There may be other components or functions added by other scrum teams. It is thus essential that your team understand where they are in the value stream. These teams may or may not be working in Agile. Your team may need something from another team or another team may need something your team produces. That said, if all teams can be synchronized it will be much more profitable. That is when a scrum of scrum comes into the picture.

Objectives of Scrum of Scrum

A scrum of scrum is the event organized with the objective of updating what is happening with other involved scrum teams. This is important as when a solution is built, often different features are built by different teams, yet they need to be combined at one point to form the complete solution.

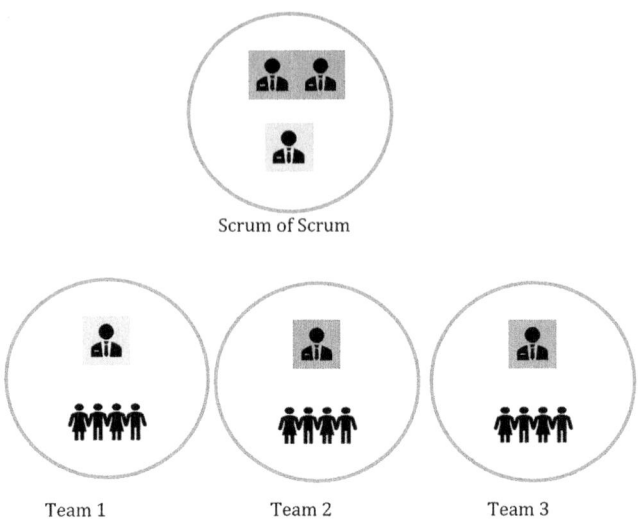

Figure 30: Scrum of Scrum

How?

Generally, the scrum of scrum will have scrum masters (or representatives) of all scrum teams coming together to give updates on behalf of their own team. You can imagine this as a standup meeting for all the involved scrum teams. It may be facilitated by a chief scrum master, Agile coach, or by any scrum master from any of the teams.

Frequency is decided by all of you. Depending on the criticality and interdependencies between teams, it may need to happen every day, every other day, or once a week. A typical duration is from fifteen minutes to one hour, depending on the number of teams and frequency of meetings. If the scrum of scrum is daily, fifteen minutes is likely sufficient, and if every other day, thirty minutes if ideal; if it happens weekly, count on one hour.

The scrum master of each scrum team represents his or her own team. As the scrum master, you need to be updated on what is happening in your team. Updates such as sprint goal, dependencies found, blockers, or impediments identified are the good updates to discuss at the scrum of the scrum. Within this meeting, you will get a good picture of what other teams are working on and their time frames, so you will likely come away with answers about interdependency problems your team has. You can even can ask for help from another team if your team has any impediments, or in turn, you might offer to help other teams.

Share the updates with your team

Once you've gathered information from other teams, share that information with your team. It will prove helpful especially if your team has any dependencies on other teams and can aid in avoiding duplication. For example, if another team is building an API or a feature, your team can simply use it without building it from scratch. Or, you can simply connect your team members with one of the teams who offered help on the impediments your team has identified. The best time to give this information or share knowledge is at the standup. Just like other team members give their updates, you can share by saying, "Yesterday I attended scrum of the scrum and found Team 2 is developing a mobile app for the product. And Rahul offered to send a software engineer from his team to discuss the continuous integration capabilities we can build together."

Be the change you want to see in your teams

What if there is no scrum of a scrum in your setup and you know that there are multiple teams working on the same value stream? This can happen where Agile is new to the organization and experience with it is reduced. In such a situation, you can set this up. Just get together with the scrum masters and start it as an initiative. Along the way, you can discuss cadence, duration, and frequency but start somewhere.

CHAPTER 10

Scrum master responsibilities after the project

Now that the project is completed, and the product you delivered is probably in use, is the scrum master's job really finished? The answer is 'probably not'.

There are few things yet to be done before one really completes the project. Below are few things to think about once the project is finished.

Celebrate

You and your team have come a long way. The team must have faced many challenges and now those are behind you. Even if the project was not a new Agile experiment, every product is something new and now that product has been delivered. You must have been running this journey for three months, six months, or maybe a year. It is something to be proud of and to be happy about, so have a celebration.

Get together with the team, your customers, and all the stakeholders with whom you have been working and have a blast. You can find a sponsor; most of the time it is just a matter of asking managers, leaders, or customers, all of whom are usually very supportive—and appreciative of the fact that you took the lead on organizing the party. Invite them too.

Go out, play some games, and eat wonderful food. Then, dance it off.

Do a retrospective on the entire project

You are already familiar with retrospectives since the team does one at the end of every sprint. You do not normally engage any external parties at the retrospectives, but now that the project is finished, it is a good time to do a retrospective while engaging other stakeholders as well.

For example, you have likely been working with project managers, PMOs, suppliers, or third parties. You can do a retrospective on the entire project by asking the question "What worked?" and, "What did not work?" Imagine starting another project to spark discussion about what you would do differently. This will be a good learning exercise for other projects to come.

Do a self-reflection

How did you do as the scrum master? What did you do well? What should you change? What do you want to start doing? How would the team evaluate your performance? What would your mentor/coach say about you? What is your Agile maturity rating now? There are many things one can learn about him or herself after the project is completed.

Self-reflection is a good starting point, because most of the time we do know that certain things worked well and some facilitation events did go badly. Write these down. And, if you that certain things that did not work, consider what you can do to improve the next project.

Then seek feedback from others. Your team members can be your best teachers. Ask them how you did: do they think you really helped them or could you have done certain things differently? Ask them and they will tell you. Most importantly, do not try to defend or justify if they report something that does not align with your expectations. For example, if you are thinking that you facilitated very well but your team members are saying that "Actually you micro-managed," don't try to defend your position. Doing so negates the whole point of asking for feedback, and you will never grow or learn a thing. Remember, this is their perspective, and it is important for you to understand how they felt and what they expected from you. Only then can you become a good servant leader.

Then ask for feedback from other stakeholders, project sponsors, customers, and product owners.

After collecting that date, you are able to build a plan to improve and you can discuss that with your mentor/coach.

Update your community of practice

Agile is not a destination. It is a journey; it is imperfect so that it can be perfected along the way. That is exactly how different Agile frameworks and practices were founded, and that is how Agile gets better and better over time.

That is the evolution. We apply what we think are the best practices, then learn that they are not working, and then we seek necessary change. To do that we need to learn and admit what works and what doesn't so that we can move forward with effecting alterations. That is where professional input from those who practice Agile every day comes into play.

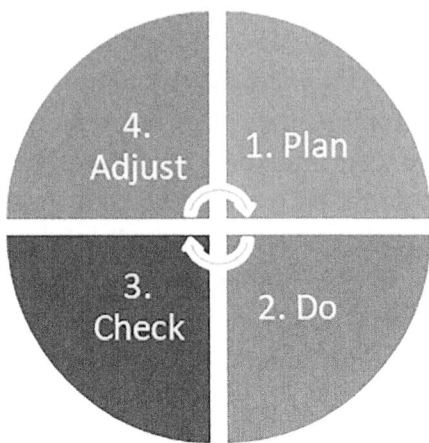

Figure 31 : PDCA cycle

In our working environments, different companies use different frameworks. However, even with the same framework, the application may be different, because companies, products, and people are different. And what we find is that some frameworks simply will not work in a given situation, while some frameworks or practices are a perfect fit. Just imagine that you as a scrum master are now going through a rough time, and if you had known another who had gone through something similar, it's likely that hours of your agony could have been avoided. The Agile community of practice comes into the picture here.

Agile Community Of Practice (COP)

Agile is about collaboration, people, and delivering value. That alone stands as good reason for us to contribute to the community and to learn from other's experiences. At the same time, we pick up new things from others and try them out ourselves, then report whether or not it was successful. This is our practice and we have to contribute and collaborate to make it better.

Agile have a pretty good community of practice. Most of the Agile practitioner's get together and share knowledge. Some write blogs, and others make social media videos. Some organize meet-ups and some host conferences. Whatever the channel they select, it is a good cause and we as practitioners need that close bonding and dependence on one another.

As a scrum master who is practicing Agile, you can contribute to this community by sharing your knowledge so that others can learn from your experience. Take part in this community by attending conferences, webinars, and meet-ups and ask your team to participate in those events as well.

If you are working in a big organization which has few scrum masters, product owners, and Agile teams, you can set up your own internal community of practice. It would be helpful for each of the practitioners to learn from each other. Sometimes one just needs a helping hand. As an example, ask another scrum master in the community to conduct the retrospective for your team. And you can do same in return. In that way, your team may not suffer the monotony of getting retrospectives from you all the time, and maybe your friend introduces a different retrospective format. That can be so much fun.

Different Agile frameworks have given enough guidance on either implementing or partaking in the community of practice. In the Spotify framework, they talk about Agile chapters for Agile practitioners. Scaled Agile Framework introduces Communities Of Practice (COP). You can read the details of SAFe COP at https://www.scaledagileframework.com/communities-of-practice

CHAPTER 11

Traits of a Scrum Master

W E HAVE DISCUSSED responsibilities of a scrum master but becoming a very good one requires a broad skill set. You can earn some of these skills from the outside world, and Agile knowledge on frameworks, principles, and responsibilities during different parts of the project are things one can get coached on—and can improve upon—over a period of time.

Apart from those skills, some of your personal qualities may prove helpful toward becoming a successful scrum master. I call these traits. Some of them you may already possess, and some you may not. If you do have these traits, you can continue to use them, while the traits you lack can be built in and further developed.

Below are some of the traits that I believe one needs to cultivate in order to be a good scrum master.

Courage

A scrum master is the main person who helps the team build new practices. And introducing something new is never easy. You may have to try new things. You may even fail. Considering the fact that a scrum master is a servant leader and a change agent, he or she needs to bring an extra dose of courage.

Not just the team but managers and customers will challenge you and may not buy what you are selling. So, it takes ample courage to face that challenge and to understand their point of view then showcase the right way. You need the courage to say, "No" nicely when faced with some of the old practices and while introducing new ones. Have the courage to say, "No" to the product owner when he or she asks you to write down user stories during every sprint. You should have the courage to coach the product owner and explain why he or she is the one who needs to write the user stories.

Courage to change yourself

You should have enough courage to change yourself, to let go of your ego. You may have to self-organize yourself, and you need courage to change your old habits and start new ones. For example, you may need to learn to speak less. One of my students in an Agile training once told me that it took him eighteen months to change that behavior, as he used to be a 'talker,' but becoming a scrum master required that he listen more.

Leadership

There is a difference between being driven and driving. If you are a good leader, your team will follow you. If you are a great leader, your team members will become leaders, since you have naturally been building leaders. If you look at people like Mahatma Gandhi, it's clear they did not have power given by the authorities. Gandhi did not try to gain power; his words were soft and his eyes were filled with compassion. Still, he wielded the power to make the entire nation follow him, to believe in him for the greater good. Watch this video if you like knowing his story. https://www.youtube.com/ watch?v=hpZwCRInrgo (Search in your tube Mahatma Gandhi - dying for freedom)

Another side of leadership is building leaders. As a scrum

master, you should build leaders. One of the objectives of Agile is building autonomy. The team should make their own decisions, take accountability of success or failure, and decide on their own action. You need to show team members that they are leaders. If you are a good leader, you will build leaders, not followers.

Peter Drucker has offered many lessons to aspirant leaders. He came up with the 'knowledge worker' philosophy and managed to infuse the seed in many manager's mindsets. I would his books to gain more insights to the concept of knowledge workers.

Books to read on leadership:

- Five Dysfunctions of a Team : Patrick M. Lencioni
- Leading at the Edge : Rachael Robertson
- Leaders eat Last: SimonSinek
- Start with Why: SimonSinek
- The Toyota Way to Lean Leadership: Jeffrey Liker, Gary L. Convis, et al.
- Leadership Agility: William B. Joiner and Stephen A. Josephs
- Together is Better: Simon Sinek
- HBR Must Read on Leadership : Harvard Business Review, Peter F. Drucker, et al.

Listening

Listening is actively engaging with a voice, with the person. We listen to understand what the other person is saying. When we do that, it changes something within us. It may be that we learn something, and that something may be about the situation or the person. Again, which one are you good at?

As a good servant leader, you need to be a good 'listener.' You will be exercising this trait many times along the way while playing the role of scrum master.

Listening at Agile ceremonies

At stand-ups, you need to listen in order to understand what impediments the team is facing. Make an effort to understand what they say by focusing on the tone of voice, for example. You may find that team members are really frustrated about the impediment, so your first reactive action needs to be to cheer them up, offer them full support, and then quickly find that support.

You even need to listen to the silence. In other words, some team members may not be speaking, so you must be able to figure out who those are and find a way to engage them.

Constant learning

When you are a true leader, you realize how little you know about most things. That realization opens up a desire to learn across areas that could prove applicable to the job you are doing.

Why do we need to learn?

When you are a scrum master, you wear multiple hats. You are:

- Process change agent – Agile process
- Behavioral change agent – behavioral changes required in the Agile project
- A servant leader
- A teacher
- A coach
- A mentor

If you look closely, these are different subject areas, so your personal interest in learning these subjects will definitely make you a successful scrum master.

At the same time, Agile is constantly refreshing. New things are added and existing things are modified based on the learning. Ten years ago in the software development process, for example, we did not discuss DevOps (Development and Operations), but now DevOps is main stream. Frameworks like SAFe constantly look to the learning of those who practice it, and they add these components to the framework. SAFe 4.0 and 4.5 reveal added DevOps and User Experience in their frameworks.

Constant learning is essential to figuring out the best practices and to being up-to-date.

How to learn

Luckily, we are in an era where education comes across many avenues. Based on the areas in which you have interest, there may be many channels for you as below:

Formal trainings

There is much training organized relevant to the areas you want to study. If you want to learn scrum master in details, there are many scrum master training opportunities. There are many sessions for learning about different Agile frameworks as well, like LeSS fundamentals.

Find out what training you need and how to engage in them.

Online trainings

One of the best things happening in this era are the many possibilities to take advantage of technology, and training opportunities abound online

LinkedIn offers online training, for example: I have seen many Agile trainings published in the Linkedin online training space. One such training is called Scrum Basics by Kelly O'Connell. There are also many other trainings built around Agile fundamentals, such as scrum master preparation and DevOps, all in the same LinkedIn space. Most of these are offered for free. Just conduct a search like 'LinkedIn Agile training' and you will be surprised with a list of available courses.

Other options are online training providers like Udemy and Lynda. Udemy offers over 80,000 courses, some of which are free and some offered for a small fee. The advantage is that you can do these courses regardless of where are you are located. As long as you have a computer and an internet connection, location is not a problem.

Books

Similar to online contents, there are many books about the subjects you want to learn. If it is about Agile, there are many options. There are also many books about leadership, and all are great sources of information. If you are serious about becoming a good scrum master, it's imperative to start gathering information through this channel.

Below is a list of books you must have in your reading list:

- Running Lean: Iterate from Plan A to Plan That Works: Ash Maurya

- Scrum: The Art of Doing Twice the Work in Half the Time: Jeff Sutherland

- The Phoenix project: A Novel About IT, DevOps and Helping Your Business Win: Gene Kim

- The Lean Startup: How Constant Innovation Creates a Radically Successful Business: Eric Ries

- EssentialScrum: A Practical Guide to the Most Popular Agile Practice: Kenneth S. Rubin

- Scrum: A Breathtaking Brief and Agile Introduction: Chris Sims and Hilary Louise Johnson

- The Scrum Field Guide: Practical Advice for Your First Year: Mitch Lacey

- Lean Analytics: Use Data to Build a Better Startup Faster: Alistair Croll and Benjamin Moskowitz

- Impact Mapping: Making a Big Impact with Software Products and Projects: GojkoAdzic

- Succeeding with Agile: Software Development Using Scrum: Mike Cohn

- Agile Product Management with Scrum: Creating Products that Customers Love: Roman Pichler

- Agile Software Development:Principles, Patterns and Practices: Robert C. Martin

- Agile Project Management: Creating Innovative Products: Jim Highsmith

- Scrum: A Revolutionary Approach to Building Teams, Beating Deadlines and Boosting Productivity: Jeff Sutherland

- Peopleware: Productive, Projects and Teams: Tom DeMarco and Tim Lister

Persistence

The Oxford Dictionary defines 'Persistence' as "the fact of continuing in an opinion or course of action in spite of difficulty or opposition." There is a reason I identified this trait as one a scrum Master needs to have. As a change agent of Agile, the ride is not going to be easy, and that is where persistence comes into the picture.

Do you believe in Agile practices? This is the first step to developing persistence for doing this job. Ask these questions of yourself: "Why you do this job? Do you believe in Agile principles and in Agile practices?" If the answer is "No," I would say it is best for you to find your passion elsewhere. And it is okay to *not* believe in this, but if that is the case, this job will become torture to you rather than motivation to succeed.

I had one senior manager who emerged from a Six-Sigma background. She found it difficult to develop the servant leadership and was constantly criticizing Agile practices. She had taken the job just because it would help her climb the corporate ladder as the organization was moving into Agile, but she did not really believe in Agile practices. Since she carried the baggage of "Six Sigma is the best," she was not open to learning the new thing as well. That said, she was doing the job for the sake of doing the job. The result was that she dumped that pressure on the team. She was simply unable to be a servant leader. She thought of the team as a self-organized unit that should be able to tackle impediments and blockers without asking for her support. In the end, she built friction between herself and the team.

Agile is a mindset change. Not everyone is going to understand these practices, so there will be resistance; when that happens, you must exhibit persistence. And if you believe in what you do, then you will not be discouraged. You will not break down but instead be motivated to find out why things are not working and to find a better way.

Innovation

Recently I conducted a SAFe Agile Scrum Master training session for one of the companies I worked for. One student who worked as a scrum master said that he faced the challenge that his team was always complaining about retrospectives. As a result, his team wanted to not conduct them. Then, we did a root cause analysis of why his team found the retrospectives to be a 'waste.' What we realized was that he had been conducting the retrospective using the same format of asking, "What is working?" and "What is not working?" then asking about what to improve—and he had been using that formula for nearly four months . Who would not be bored?

This is where innovation comes into the picture. We need to constantly look into the ways of doing improvements. Suppose the team was doing manual testing. How can they make it efficient? To find better ways we need to think differently and challenge ourselves. It takes relentless effort to make the things better.

Innovation needs to be applied at the individual as well as a team level. That means as the scrum master you need to find new, interesting ways to perform your duties. In the above example of retrospectives becoming wasteful events, the scrum master should have treated this as a problem to solve. Rather than jumping into the solution of "Let's not conduct retrospectives anymore," do a root cause analysis of why the retrospectives are deemed wasteful and prompt the team for ideas about how to make them "productive events." Then we will likely find many solutions, not just one.

Going beyond the individual level, you need to influence teams, and programs need to be innovative as well. Frameworks like Scaled Agile enforces this by allocating at regular intervals (Program Increment) for innovation. Within that iteration (two weeks), teams individually and collectively organize problem-solving workshops to find out which problems to prioritize and solve. Events like problem solving workshops and hackathons are organized during this period

You need to be an innovator up to a certain level. When you are an innovator, you become a problem solver, and you need to be an innovator for the team as well as for yourself.

CHAPTER 12

The Scrum Master's Toolbox

IN THE PREVIOUS chapters we discussed the different roles a scrum master plays. Facilitator is one of those roles. When you play the role of the facilitator you must facilitate many Agile ceremonies, trainings, and coaching sessions and when doing so, certain items come in handy. I call this the 'scrum master's toolbox.' Many items can be in that toolbox to come to your rescue in certain situations. Below are a few things to note:

Stationery

When I get into a project, one of the first things I do is prepare my own stationery box. That is irrespective of whether I am facilitating events or not. Even at normal meetings, I try to be colloborative. That is where at least a bunch of post-it notes and Sharpies come into the picture. When prepared, you don't need to run around searching for post-it notes. Having an array of stationery is never going to disappoint you.

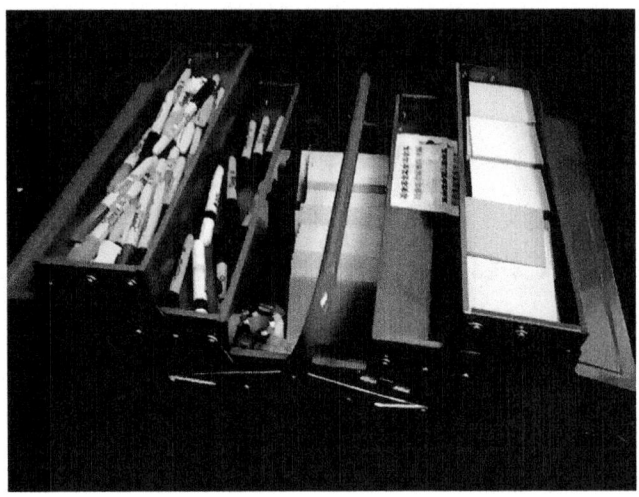

Figure 32 : Scrum master's tool box

Below is a list of items you might consider having in your toolbox:

- Post-it notes
- Sharpies
- Pens
- Whiteboard markers
- Index cards
- Duct tape
- Blutack
- Rulers
- Voting dots from different colors
- Ping pong/tennis balls
- Flip charts
- Kudo cards

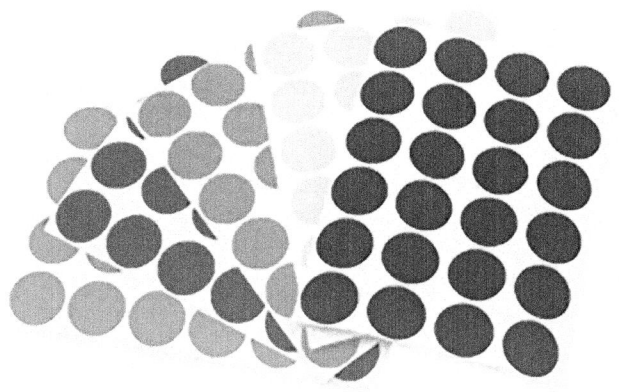

Figure 33: Voting dots

Figure 34: Duct tape

Figure 35: Blu Tack

If you were wondering what the ping pong/tennis ball is for, I found it a vital tool to controlling meetings especially during standups. You can pass the ping pong ball to the person who is allowed to talk. Passing the ball is a fun activity and at the same time brings disciplines to the team as they do not disturb the person talking.

Poker cards

Almost all scrum teams are familiar with relative estimation. Efforts of implementing a user story are estimated using the relative estimation. Planning poker is one tool we use to estimate user stories using story points. If you have attended any scrum master training, there is a good chance that you already own few packs of poker cards. Otherwise, these packs are now available for purchase online and they are an essential tool for your toolbox.

Figure 36: Poker cards

Retrospective templates

As we discussed previously one of the key ceremonies in Agile is the sprint retrospectives. It is essential to conduct one at the end of every sprint.

If you conduct the retrospectives in the same way every time, team members complain that they are useless. It's important to be innovative when it comes to conducting retrospectives.

One option is that you have a series of retrospective themes, stories, and games representing different team maturities. Normally in a retrospective, we discuss what worked well, what did not work well, and what we need to start doing. But if you repeat the at every sprint, you are not going to get the team's full attention. But, if you come up with a story like below, you might find success:

"Okay folks, two weeks ago we hopped into this tiny little boat called sprint and all of us were sailing towards the sunny island of 'delivering payment gateway to our customers.' We raised the sail high and started towards the sunny island. But, oh shit, what happened in the middle of the trip? (Consider adding some action, or some sound to depict that the team got caught up in a storm or caught up in a powerful supportive wind.) Remember we were caught up in strong winds from time to time and we could actually sail faster without much effort? And the days were sunny right? Okay, let's write down what made our sprint faster and better."

Now you can direct the team to write down what went well in the sprint. Once the writing on post-it notes is finished, you can direct them to paste the post-it on the poster.

Then you can continue: "Okay, then remember what happened the other day? I am sure you remember. Oh, it was painful, right? Bang. We hit a rock, right? Remember what a tragedy it was? Okay, let's write down what made us slow in the last sprint."

I believe you get the idea now. You can make this dramatic by being creative, by creating new posters, and making new stories. Make it fun. That is why I mention that when you play the scrum master role, you have to play many roles, and this one is one of them. Actually, it gives you the opportunity to be creative and to think differently, which is how you build your style. One of my scrum masters came up with the below retrospective story and it was actually fun when he told this story of going to the moon in the final sprint.

Figure 37 : A retrospective template

Feature /user story templates

One key area where the team usually struggles is when writing user stories. This issue is obvious when the team is new to Agile and has no previous exposure to writing user stories. Due to that, it seems difficult at the start, and the team will try to get away from the format of user stories. I believe in the fact that it needs to make sense to the team, however, ignoring the components like acceptance criteria and definition of done can be an issue later in the project. It will be your job to get the team into the practice of writing the user stories, complete with the required it required. As we know, the way in which user stories are written is beneficial to the team as well as to the product owner, so you need to make it happen. The simplest way to do this is come up with a template.

I created the template below, printed it on multi-coloured A4 paper, and cut it for use by the team.

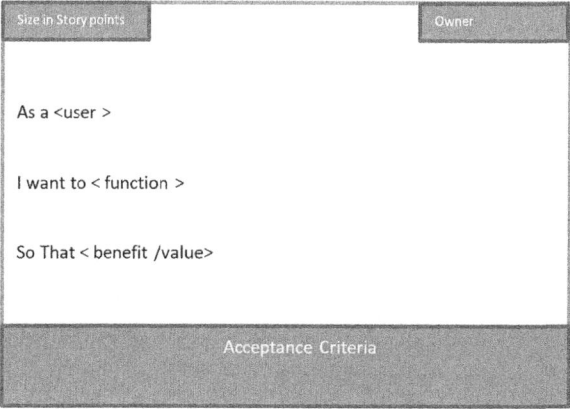

It was so effective that at every sprint planning, team members used to ask the product owner "What is the definition of done?" , because it was there in the template. You can be more creative here by printing stickers or post-it notes with the needed templates and make them ready for your team.

Team building games

This book highlighted the importance of team building in a few places. Of course, what makes Agile different from any other methodologies is that it allows autonomy in the team so that the team is motivated to deliver value to the customer. This is easier said than done. We can group seven to nine team members with a scrum master and a product owner and start an Agile project, but it does not guarantee that the team is going to deliver any value soon. Conflicts are going to happen, and we always find one or two members who think differently and will try to work against the tide.

Team building activities and games come into the picture when we discuss this aspect of building teams. It is important that team building activities are conducted regularly. It helps the team to get united and work together for something other than work. Speaking personally, team building activities have always helped me to find better people. Competitions, job security, hierarchies, job grades, and salary scales cause them to treat team members differently. But team building activities help them move away from that and build a secure environment.

You can have a list of such team building activities and games in your toolbox for which you can pull time for depending on what status the team is in. Ice-breaking activities and team bonding games such as beer pong or cricket or hiking during the weekends, or even a marshmallow challenge are really helpful to bring unity to a team.

Training materials

The scrum master is the ambassador who promotes Agile. He or she makes sure that rest of the organization understands how the team is working and what Agile principles they are following, which in turn explains how the rest of the organization should support the journey. This is an important action to gaining the support required from the organization. This will help to reduce the negative force coming from outside the team.

In preparation for that at any time, you should have a list of the readymade set of presentation decks/training materials which could be used for different occasions, depending on the objective and the audience.

Below are the different scenarios you can consider when preparing presentation decks:

Objective	Audience	What should it include
• Give an overview of Agile and benefits • Introduce Agile to the rest of the managers of your interactions • Learning opportunity for others in a different way of operating	Managers, PMOs, Project Managers, Stakeholders who will be interacting with your project	• Why Agile is required • The difference between traditional software development vs. Agile Delivery • Benefits of Agile delivery • Brief on Agile manifesto/ principles /practices (like time boxing /increments, etc.) • Different Agile frameworks • The framework you are going to operate • What is expected from the managers/leaders (be clear about the leadership style/autonomy your tea need to have, etc.)

Objective	Audience	What should it include
• Setting up the operational structure • Managing expectations	IT Operations team Stakeholders of the project PMO Other managers who have any influence like project managers, program managers, Customer	• Your team structure • Roles in your team and team members profiles with photos, etc. • The problem you are solving (get product owners to present this part) • Product features • Product roadmap • Team cadence • Stakeholder expectations • How stakeholders should interact with the team • What stakeholders should not do. For example, not put pressure on the team and remain realistic in terms of releases, how the team members should not be allocated to other projects, etc.

Objective	Audience	What should it include
• Project KPIs	PMO, Program manager, Customer, Team	• Your template decks should include below and every time you present or are requested to present, they should be refreshed with the latest data: • Epic burndown chart • Feature burndown the chart • Sprint burn down chart etc.

CHAPTER 13

Visual Kanban Wall

ABC Bank (a fictitious name) decided to introduce Agile to the organization and they selected a pilot product. Team members were selected and they in turn appointed a manager to be product manager and another three managers to act as product owners. Team members were picked from the different functional divisions and assigned to the three teams, but they did not have the Agile capability in the bank so they hired a scrum master who brought the necessary experience. Management asked the scrum master to support all three teams and the product owners.

The scrum master suggested to the three product owners that they must start creating a product backlog. He explained how the requirements should be written using the user story format, and he helped them by writing a few user stories. Then the scrum master suggested that they create the product backlog in 'Jira.' Neither the product owners nor the team members had ever heard about Jira, so then the scrum master gave them a demonstration. They were impressed, and they wanted to try it.

The scrum master was very happy, so he created Jira accounts for everybody, gave them access, then provided them training. They asked the product owners to create their user stories in the product backlog in Jira board. They met the next day and the scrum master projected his computer onto the television in the room. The scrum master sat near the television while rest of the team members (around thirty team members from all three teams) all sat around the big table.

Now the product backlog was up on the television and the scrum master had the computer keyboard. He then asked each of the product owners to explain the user stories. The product owner asked the scrum master, "Mark, can you zoom in? I cannot see."

"Ah, let me try," said the Scrum Master. He managed to zoom in then he said,"This is the maximum. Is it okay?" The others nodded, but someone at the end of table said, "Sorry, I cannot read it. Can you read it out loud please?"

"Oh sure." The Scrum master then read it out loud.

Then the Scrum master looked at the product owner and said, "Well, actually this user story is no longer valid. Can you please delete it and write this user story?" Mark then started reading the user story and the scrum master did the typing.

People at the end of the room could not clearly see what the new user story was because it was not large enough to be visible to far out in the room.

They spent three hours in that room and at the end of the session team members hardly remembered the user stories or what they had to work on.

What is a visual Kanban wall?

One of the mostly frequently asked questions in Agile trainings is, "What is the best tool to use?" What they mean most of the time is what digital tool is most useful in Agile sessions. Often I answer this by asking another question. "Are your team members in different geographical locations?"

If the answer is "No," then I say, "Then you do not need a digital tool," and my experience has not proven otherwise. The only tool such teams need is a visual Kanban wall.

The visual Kanban wall is one of the best tools an Agile team can have. We call it a visual performance indicator as the Kanban wall passes so much information without producing any reports.

Visual Performance Indicators

A well-designed Kanban wall indicates ample information such as suggested below:

- The development workflow
- What is the scope of the current sprint?
- How many user stories are in the current sprint?
- How big/complex are the user stories?
- Who is working on what?
- The remaining user stories in the product backlog
- User stories with any impediments
- Completed work

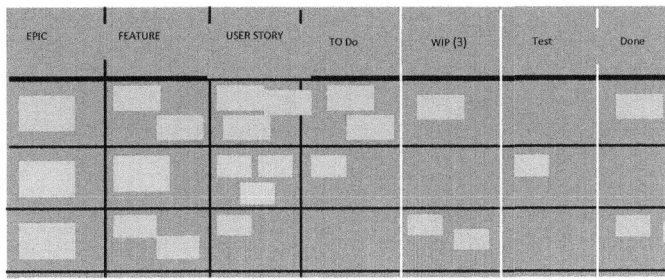

Figure 38: Visual Kanban wall of a development team

Power of Visual Kanban Wall

The visual Kanban Wall is not just a tool to display task flow.

What I have noticed is that teams who use visual Kanban walls are more collaborative, happier, and more productive. I believe face-to-face communication among team helps accomplish all of that. Also, since the talking is based on the user stories or tasks displayed on the board, it helps to focus the discussion.

It is readily available. It is visible all the time. It can be explained to anyone at any time. For example, if one of the managers asks about progress on a particular user story, you simply check where it is on the Kanban wall. If the user story is in the 'To Do' column, work has yet to begin. The Kanban wall simply reflects the actual, current situation.

Uses of Visual Kanban wall

To display the best uses of a visual Kanban wall, I will pull from an example related to SAFe framework. After the PI planning, all teams create a program Kanban wall and it looks like this:

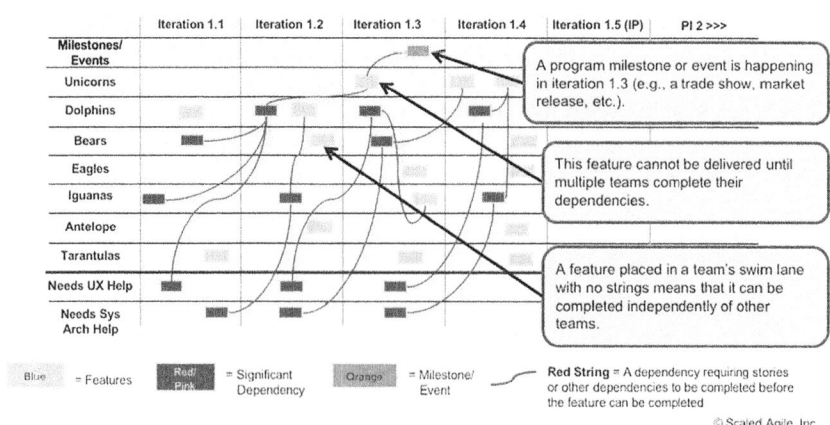

Figure 39: Dependencies (ScaledAgileFramework.com)

Above is a program Kanban board which has been created during the PI planning. It showcases user stories, where the red strings between them represent dependencies among user stories. This is visible to anyone, so it is easy to figure out who is dependent on whom, then it triggers discussions toward finding a solution.

Limitations of Kanban walls

Visual Kanban walls are the best way to radiate information and to increase team collaboration. Their implementation is simple and takes little effort to create and maintain. And it is free. There is no license cost attached to it (like many digital tools). However, it poses some limitations, but when aware of them, you can find a way around them.

However, visual Kanban walls are difficult to implement and maintain. One must be mindful of the limitations so that they can be avoided.

- **Poor practices on updating the Kanban wall**:

    One limitation we see all the time is that the team does not update the board regularly. They may have finished the work but the visual Kanban wall does not say so because it has not been updated. It takes practice, and as scrum master you must get the team to do this regularly. One of the best ways to do so is to require team members to move the cards while they are giving standup updates. Once the team members get the rhythm, they will update it regularly, but until you get to that point, plan on repeating the order.

- **It is not movable**:

    If you place the Kanban wall on a physical wall, it cannot be moved to any place you want it. This can be a problem if the team does not have a dedicated room or workplace. For meetings, if you must go to different rooms every day, and if the Kanban wall cannot be moved, then the team may find it difficult.

There are a few solutions.

First, try to get a dedicated workplace for your team. We discussed this in previous chapters. The Kanban wall needs to be in that workplace, and for that, the team needs to have one. You should talk to your managers and get their support for this, then create the Kanban wall there.

The second option is to get a movable board and mount the Kanban wall on it.

One alternative is to use movable boards. For example, try a movable partition board like in Figure 40 below. This board works like a whiteboard and both sides of it are usable. Since it is mounted on wheels and it's lightweight, it can be dragged into any place. Stationery shops have these boars in different sizes, and this may be the ideal solution.

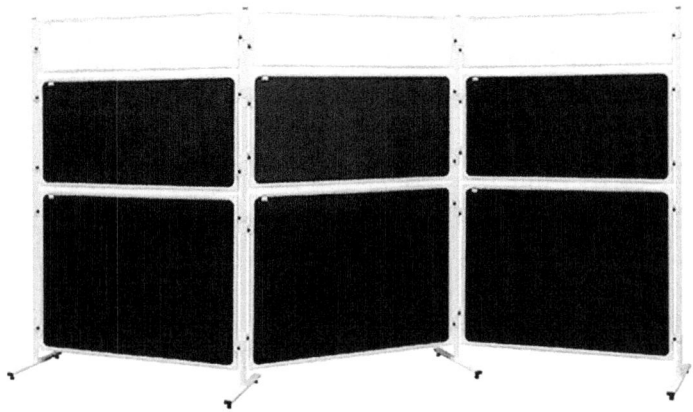

Figure 40 : Movable board

- **Cannot be accessible remotely**:

  Since the Kanban wall is in a fixed place it is not possible to access it from a remote location. If your team is a distributed team with members in different locations, then a Kanban wall in a fixed place can be a limitation. However, if we go back to basics when we create these small teams, we can encourage getting team members co-located, because coordination, synchronization, and communication among team members in different geographical locations can be difficult. The full benefit of Agile is hardly achieved when team members are in different locations, for example, if one member is in Australia, another in Singapore, and yet another in India. The first thing to do is to fix that problem.

But, if your team is part of a bigger program with many scrum teams in different locations, then you fall into the distributed Agile category. In that case, using a digital tool would be a benefit.

Now, if perhaps one day one of your team members may work from home, you do not need to go digital just for that. Those are exceptions as your team members do not work from home all the time. Discuss with the team the best way to tackle such situations.

CHAPTER 14

Distributed Agile

THERE IS ONE thing with which all Agile practitioners agree: Agile works best in the co-located environment. When we analyze which teams produced the best outcomes, and who had the best team morale, we always found they were co-located. We thus conclude that to get the best outcomes from Agile, teams need to be co-located.

Most of the time, however, reality says otherwise. Recently I was consulted for a project with members from four different citifies in two countries, and that company wanted to implement a Scaled Agile Framework in that project.

Within this shrinking world, it is inevitable that we must work seamlessly across a wide geography, with different partners, and for different customers. We have to brainstorm ways to collaborate with distributed teams, although the mechanism to do so is not yet nailed down. However, a few best practices as below exisit.

1. **Always try to co-locate the teams**:

   This is our best practice. If there is an opportunity to influence the team structure, always suggest resourcing the team members from the same location. This option can be difficult, and sometimes it can prove costly as well. Still, it will prove the most productive in the long run.

2. **Create small teams at each geographical location**:

    If number one above is unsuccessful due to various reasons, try creating small teams at each location. Avoid creating teams with members from different locations.

    Give the ownership of the product features or user stories to each team so that the dependencies from each team at each different location are minimal. However, always keep them synchronized through some virtual sessions as all features/user stories do belong to one product.

3. **Start with a team building workshop**:

    At least at the beginning of the project, co-locate all teams and kick off with a discovery session that includes a project vision, product vision discovery, and an Agile training on how they are going to work together. Include team building activities as part of the discovery session.

    If possible, arrange to kick off the project at one location and bring all team members to the same place. It sounds like a big investment to arrange such an event, but it pays off. If the team forms a good bonding, regardless of location, they will help each other pull it off when things get rough. Personal connections built within this first week definitely help to recover from rough patches.

4. **Use the technology to bridge geographical barriers**:

    When I was in global organization, I was responsible for a regional product portfolio. Regardless that my team and I had to work with team members in India, UK, China, US, Kuwait, and Qatar, the company policy did not allow us to use webcams or any other video conferencing mechanisms. Doing Agile in that kind of environments is impractical. We cannot expect the benefits of Agile in such environments.

Discuss with your managers about logistics and infrastructure you need to run Agile with distributed teams. Explain to them the benefits and difficulties of not having the proper infrastructure.

It is required to have some face-to-face communication. A room with a video conferencing facility, computers with webcams, and instant messaging facilities are the least what you need. It is your job to discuss this with the relevant parties like PMOs and seniors so that they understand the requirements.

However, in the worst-case scenarios make sure that expectations are set properly.

5. **Identify the overlapping time and make the team available during that period**:

   Time zone differences can be a killer in distributed teams. When one team is coming to the office at one location, the other may be preparing to go home at the end of the day. Just identify the time frame where all team members are in office, then arrange all the ceremonies during this overlapping time.

6. **Use digital tools**:

   If the team is made up of team members from different locations, it is worthwhile to invest in a digital collaboration tool. Although I said previously that physical Kanban walls are the best, digital tools come into the picture in a distributed team due to the fact that a physical wall may not be shared by everyone on the team. Such tools include Trello, Jira, Asana, and VerionOne. There are many tools available online, but each may differ based on the pricing and product features.

7. **Include the remote members in Agile ceremonies**:

Being in a remote location should not be a barrier to
including team members in Agile ceremonies like sprint
planning, sprint reviews, or sprint retrospectives. In fact,
you must include them in all of those ceremonies as they
will feel left out and unmotivated otherwise.

Make sure that they are part of sprint reviews (showcases).
Even though they are in a different location, they can
still present their user stories in action. This will make a
huge difference to them as they can get direct feedback
from the customer rather than having you present their
behalf, in which case customer feedback is passed to them
via you.

In one previous project we had a distributed team. The
scrum master and product owner were in Australia at the
client site, and the development team was in India. Before
Agile was properly implemented, the product owner used
to talk to the customer and product backlog was created
by him. Then the scrum master set up the sprint planning
with the offshore team where the product owner would
present the backlog stories. All commutation happened
only via a product owner or the scrum master. As a
result, the client did not even know the names of the
offshore team, and the offshore team did not know the
client by name. Due to many reasons, this was not the
right setup.

Then within one sprint, we changed this model. We
removed the middle men between the two teams and
appointed the product owner from the business side as part
of the team. The offshore team members were authorized
to connect directly with the client to get more details or to

ask them to test. The client passed feedback directly to the development team in Mumbai. They build a good rapport and soon started producing a shippable product at the end of every sprint (because the waste in the value stream was nil).

The next shift came with the sprint review/showcase. The client was invited to the showcase, and the team members in Mumbai presented the working software of the user story on which each of them worked. True, their English was not perfect, and their presentation skills were not perfect in the beginning because they were nervous. They used to be a behind-the-curtain type and when the opportunity came to talk directly to the client, they became shy. That is where the job of the scrum master comes into play. He or she can explain to the client and assure the team that they are doing great, as well as fill in gaps if required. Once the client understood that the barriers did not stop the team from producing a great quality product, the client was calm. In fact, they were thrilled that they could finally see the masterminds behind this solution. They could see the faces (via video conferencing) of these young, motivatedworkers. On the other side, the development team understood what this solution meant to the client. How critical was it? They heard the client directly, which motivated them to do better in the next sprint, and there was no information lost between layers. That improves the productivity.

That made a huge difference in that project, and that team mentioned that it was one of the best projects in their career. When the project ended, they were emotional and dreaded moving on to another project that may not bring the same positive experience.

Distributed Agile is definitely a challenge. It is not ideal but sometimes the reality is that we must implement it. I try to stay away from that model, but in the worst-case scenario, we need to have a budget—and enough support – to fill the geographical gaps through technology. Be creative and you will find a way.

CHAPTER 15

Scrum Master's Day

S CRUM MASTER'S DAY is never the same. However, we can track a pattern that most scrum masters follow. Below is just an indication of one such pattern, but bear in mind that you may have a different pattern or choose different activities depending on the types and number of scrum teams you are in and your lifestyle

Below is a sample from Jim who is a scrum master at maturity level 2.

A normal day in the middle of a sprint

Time	Activity	Comment
6.00 AM	Wake up	
6.10	Coffee and read a book on Agile/blog	
6.30 -8.00	Morning routine (family/ get ready/ drop kids at school, etc.)	

Time	Activity	Comment
8.00-8.30	Commute to office Listen to podcast on Agile/lean, design thinking/leadership, etc.	
8.30 – 9.00	Check emails/daily meeting schedule/reply to emails, etc.	
9.00- 10.00	Gemba walk	Walk to each of the team members and chat about things completely unrelated to work (such as the cricket match the previous day or *Game of Thrones*.
10.00- 10.15	Standup	Gather around the Kanban wall. Greet the team. Pass the ball to one of the team members and request he or she starts the stand up.
10.15 -10.30	Follow up on the items parked during the standup.	If there was anything parked during the standup, pick that item with the respective team member and discuss what help is required.

Time	Activity	Comment
10.30 – 11.00	Identify the actions required to remove the blockers/impediments identified during the standup.	
11.00- 12.00	Follow up on any impediments.	Based on the action plan identified, reach out the product owner, PMO, program manager, and any other stakeholder who has to act on the impediments.
12.00-12.30	Exercise	Running/going to the gym with a friend/team members
12.30-1.15	Have lunch with a team member who needs coaching.	Use this time to coach any of the team members whom you identified as having some blockers/ impediments or limitations. Probably this team member has expressed that he likes to talk to you so you can utilize this time if it is okay with the team member.

Time	Activity	Comment
1.15- 2.15	Product owner discussion	Product owner has requested help in terms of upcoming release. Scrum master is discussing where he can help the product owner.
2.15-2.45	Scrum of scrum	Scrum master walks to the program Kanban wall and meets the other scrum masters to give update on his team.
2.45 – 3.15	Coffee with the Agile coach	Scrum Master meets the Agile coach and discusses issues he is facing and gets some coaching.
3.15-3.45	Visit to the Kanban wall to check out what needs attention tomorrow. Check whether the product backlog is groomed by the product owner and whether it is ready for the upcoming refinement session.	

Time	Activity	Comment
3.45-4.30	• Check emails/replies • Check confirmations from the invitees for the upcoming sprint review. • Send reminders to those who did not yet respond. • Update the burn down chart.	
4.30	Off from work	
5.00- 6.00	Attend a meet-up	
6.00 onwards	Personal/family time	

Last day of the sprint

Time	Activity	What to expect
6.00 AM	Wake up	
6.10	Coffee and read a book on Agile/blog	
6.30 -8.00	Morning routine (family/getting ready/ drop kids at school, etc.)	
8.00-8.30	Commute to office listening to podcast on Agile/lean design thinking/leadership, etc.	

Time	Activity	What to expect
8.30 – 9.00	Check emails/daily meeting schedule/reply to emails, etc.	
9.00- 10.00	Gemba walk	Check whether team is ready to present, identify who presents what, that agenda is done, and that the meeting rooms are ready.
10.00- 11.30	Sprint Showcase/Review	• Welcome the stake-holders. • Explain the agenda. • Hand over to product owner to present the sprint goal and respective user stories. • Hand over to each team member to present the working solution of each user story. • Capture the questions asked during the showcase. • Wrap up with the Brun down chat of the sprint. • Don't forget to give kudos to the team.

Time	Activity	What to expect
11.30 -12.30	Team lunch	After the showcase go for a lunch with the team and offer them the opportunity to walk through the feedback from the stakeholders. It is a good unofficial way to understand their motivations.
12.30 – 1.30	Sprint review update	Compose a sprint update message to attendees, absentees, PMOs, Program managers, and sponsors. • If you recorded the showcase, attach the showcase link and send the update. • Follow up with those who requested more details.

Time	Activity	What to expect
1.30- 2.30	Tidy up the Kanban wall / digital tool	Discuss with the product owner and the team about actions on remaining tasks which are incomplete in the sprint. Determine what can be done during the remaining hours of the day or move to the backlog. Update the Burn down chart accordingly
3.00 – 4.00	Retrospective	
4.00- 4.30	Check the readiness for the sprint planning next week. Check emails and reply,	
4.30 – 7 (or beyond)	Team celebration	Go for a team event outside like go carting, outdoor games, tennis, or anything the team likes to do.

First day of the sprint

Time	Activity	What to expect
6.00 AM	Wake up	
6.10	Coffee and read a book on Agile/blog	
6.30 -8.00	Morning routine (family/getting ready/ drop kids at school, etc.)	
8.00-8.30	Commute to office listening to podcast on Agile/lean design thinking/leadership, etc.	
8.30 – 9.00	Check emails/check preparation for the sprint planning/team greetings	
9.00 – 12.00	Sprint Planning	
12-1.00	Lunch with the product owner/team	Catch up with product owner on what to expect in the next sprint. Discuss what dependencies/risks are anticipated.
1.00 – 2.30	Update the Kanban wall/digital tool	

Time	Activity	What to expect
2.30 – 3.30	Update the stakeholders on the current sprint goal/scope	Prepare a summary for stakeholders of the sprint goal/scope/capacity. Send the meeting invitations for upcoming backlog planning/grooming and sprint showcase sessions.
3.30- 4.30	Coach/mentor a team member who needs help.	
4.30	Off from work and family/personal time	

CHAPTER 16

Anti- Agile Patterns

A S DISCUSSED PREVIOUSLY, Agile is simple. But mastering it is a science and an art because Agile is a mindset change. It takes time and effort to master it, since it is all too easy to fall back on the old ways of working.

The scrum master's contribution in implementing Agile correctly is huge, which is why you he or she needs to be aware of anti-Agile patterns.

What is an anti-agile pattern?

You have already read the Agile manifesto, Agile principles, Agile practices, and about the scrum master's role and responsibilities. Any practice or behavior that goes against these Agile values can be clarified as part of an anti-Agile pattern. As I have mentioned, "Agile is a mindset change," and this mindset change is not going to be that easy.

"Habits are not easy to build "

Why it is important that to know anti-Agile patterns

When we practice Agile it is easy to fall back into our old patterns. As an example, not having stand-ups or skipping for one day are just a couple of pitfalls. When that happens the impact can be much more than one thinks. Once one falls back into the old pattern, it is difficult to get the rhythm back.

The scrum master knows Agile practices thoroughly and should notice when the team, product owner, or organization is falling back to the old style of working. When that happens, he or she must let everyone know, then help them to come back to Agile.

Below is a list of anti-Agile patterns which can originate from the scrum master.

1 Selecting anyone in the team as scrum master

As explained in a previous chapter, not just anyone on the team can be appointed scrum master. To be a scrum master, a certain amount of experience, Agile knowledge, and leadership instinct is required. That means that selecting anyone on the team as scrum master is just setting up the project for failure.

Just imagine that the organization is using LeSS as the framework. How can just anyone from the team be scrum master? I have seen this fail, where both scrum masters and the team struggle because of this random selection.

Selection of scrum master is an important decision and should be done wisely. Below are few guidelines to avoid this anti-pattern.

Avoiding this anti-pattern

- If the Agile project is new, let the Agile coach be the scrum master for few sprints.
- Select a team member who has already practiced Agile for some time.

- Offer the scrum master coaching by an experienced Agile coach.

- Agile training, especially the framework they are going to implement, should be mandatory.

2 Selecting project manager as scrum master

Most of the time, the project manager's job is in a controlled environment, in charge of the project budget, schedule, and scope. Doing all of that is extremely difficult. How difficult? Ask from any project manager.

Due to this pressure, most of the time project managers go to command and control mode of management. Sometimes that leads to micro-management. I remember one of my project managers giving me just one day to write, test, and deploy a web site to production early in my career. He did not have time to listen to the technical difficulties of that web site; he just wanted it to be done—and fast. I worked all night and was exhausted. On and off he came to check progress, but I felt like quitting on the spot. That is why making a project as scrum master could prove a bad choice.

Scrum masters are servant leaders, coaches, and mentors. Their job is to build high performing teams, not to give commands. It is a job which required ample patience, empathy, and a diligent selection of tactics. A project manager who has previously been in command and control mode may struggle to find this balance, not to say that it is impossible. A wise project manager will crack this code, but it will take some time.

Our experience shows that this transition is a bit difficult for most project managers unless they are committed to change themselves.

Avoiding this anti-pattern

The easiest way to avoid this anti-pattern is to avoid assigning project managers as scrum masters. Having said that, even in Agile environments, project management is sometimes required.

But if a project manager takes the leap of becoming a scrum master then Agile training should be made mandatory. Without it, the project manager will try to implement normal project manager practices in Agile teams, which can be a disaster.

Also, such scrum masters should be provided with an Agile coach who can help them realize the wrong practices and help them to cultivate the correct agile practices and mindset.

3 Combining product owner and scrum master

This anti-pattern can emerge from a traditional organization which tries to implement Agile without proper guidance. The scrum team has three roles: scrum master, product owner, and development team. There is a reason that it specifies all three roles.

Product owner responsibilities

Since you have read the responsibilities of scrum master, you have a clear understanding of the responsibilities of a product owner. Product strategy, vision, product features, roadmap, prioritizations, representing, the customer, and explaining these to the team are few. It is a full-time job with a lot on one person's shoulders, making it very difficult to do any other job to the fullest.

We have seen how Agile has been unsuccessful when the scrum master and product owner roles are combined. We will not be able to achieve the optimal levels or the outcomes by combining these roles.

Avoiding this anti-pattern

If you are a scrum master or a product owner and you were asked to perform both roles, don't try to be a superhero. Explain why it is not a good idea and talk about the cost you personally have to pay in such situations.

As a scrum master your job is to establish the right Agile process and you should be courageous enough to say, "No" whenever required, and to offer with justifications.

4 Skipping Stand-ups

This is an anti-pattern that can emerge from either the scrum master or the development team, especially when they are new to Agile.

There will be many excuses not to conduct stand-ups:

- We all know what each of us is doing.

- We are sitting at the same place, so we can talk to each other to get the updates.

- Today is a busy day, and we need this time to complete the work.

- My tasks are same as yesterday: it is the same update so I don't need to waste fifteen minutes to say that.

- I have a client meeting, so I cannot give up this time.

These are some of the things I have heard either from scrum master or from the team but for no reason should standups be missed. Read the chapter on this subject for more details.

5 Skipping Backlog refinement

Backlog refinement is done regularly as per the cadence to make sure that product backlog is up-to-date with the latest changes. Also, it adds relevant details to the remaining user stories. Most of the time backlog will be created when the project is started. But after that, backlog will not be refined since there are user stories already in the backlog; this may be an excuse to skip the backlog refinement. Another excuse is that the product owner is busy.

When that happens, the scrum master must explain to the product owner that it's imperative to establish the right practices. When it is required, the backlog refinement day can be shifted based on the busy schedules, but it can't be skipped.

Cost of not doing the backlog refinement

The cost of not doing the backlog refinement can be high. Below are few highlights:

- Sprint planning can be too long.
- Sprint planning may not result the sprint planning outcomes.
- Uncertainties of user stories can be high so the user story estimations can be high.
- Since the details and dependencies are not identified at the right time, there is a risk of not completing the user stories.

Avoiding this anti-pattern

Scrum master must make sure that backlog refinement is done as agreed in the cadence. When there is a tendency from the product owner to skip the event, coaching is required so that you can explain the costs to the product owner. Also, you can extend the helps he or she needs such as helping to come up with acceptance criteria.

6 Scrum master writing user stories

I have seen some scrum masters sitting and writing user stories very obediently. Ultimately, the product owner thinks writing user stories is a scrum master's job.

We are not talking about scrum master offering help when the team members or product owner is busy. But as a practice, if the scrum master keeps writing the user stories for the team, that becomes an anti-pattern.

User stories need to be written by the product owner primarily and the team refines them at the sprint planning session. When the scrum master is focused on writing user stories, facilitation and time boxing, which are scrum master responsibilities, may be missed and collaboration sessions can go wrong.

When this anti-pattern is about to happen, the scrum master needs to explain to the product owner and the team that it is their responsibility to write the user stories.

7 Scrum master's assignment for multiple projects

This is another anti-pattern we see from traditional organizations. Due to the resource limitations, we see scrum masters assigned to multiple projects. Depending on many things like a scrum master's experience, Agile maturity of the team, and Agile maturity of the organization, this becomes an anti-pattern.

If the scrum master is completely new to Agile and he or she is assigned to two projects, it is a recipe for failure. A new scrum master has so much to learn, so handling multiple scrum teams will not be beneficial.

When the scrum master is experienced but the team is completely new to Agile, it is another anti-pattern if the scrum master has to serve multiple teams. A scrum team that is new to Agile will be demanding much from a scrum master and availability of the scrum master is key to success. If the scrum master has to serve another such team, then both teams may not benefit as the scrum master may not be available.

However, when the teams are experienced and self-organized, scrum master can serve another team. But this is something which needs to be considered carefully by assessing each situation in turn.

CHAPTER 17

Career Progress

"WELL, AGILE IS not quite a career, right?" It was the practice lead for the tech company I was working for a few years ago. He hired me a year prior when starting up the practice and I was thrilled to join the organization, hoping to help the organization and see myself grow. I sensed the organization did not really think seriously about Agile so I was not sure where is my career heading in that organization. That was the reason I had to have a chat with my manager and clear things up.

"Is that what you think?" I answered him with a counter-question.

"Well, there is nothing beyond scrum master, right? And anyone can be a scrum master," he responded with his own counter-question.

I was unsure about whether I should have been surprised or not with that answer. Often I encounter leaders who cannot explain what is next for the scrum master. This showcases a lack of knowledge and understanding about Agile as a practice.

Due to the fact that Agile is the new kid in the industry, progression, or what is next for its practitioners, are challenging questions to most people and to organizations. However, Agile was not born yesterday. Good progress in it as a career has been made in some organizations. Although Agile career development framework is a deeper, more strategic discussion, I want to showcase the options one has if you interested in following this as a progression line.

If your passion is Agile, then as a career it is a quite a pleasant journey in terms of career progress. There are few possible branches based on the area of interest and the expertise. Below is my view on where one can grow as a scrum master. Although it is based on a corporate and enterprise level, we have huge potential as independent consultants or advisors who build up their own consultancy practice.

You become a scrum master because you have been selected based on your expertise, passion, or knowledge of Agile, or you yourself have identified as a scrum master after working in an Agile team. The latter is the case for most people. If you have been successful in a scrum team and still have the same passion and drive, your next level most of the time is to become a chief scrum master who can coordinate few scrum teams.

Chief Scrum Master

If your organization has multiple scrum teams aligned with a program of work, you likely have many scrum masters and many products owners. What I have seen is that not all scrum masters synchronize a program or one product. This malpractice can hinder the progress and productivity of your team's bigger enterprise product.

Well-organized and matured organizations arrange scrum of scrums and aim to synchronize multiple teams so the requirement of organizing and coordinating scrum of scrum arises. This is where your experience as a scrum master comes into the picture. Either you can be nominated to be chief scrum master, or you might be hired as a chief scrum master, but you need to look out for scrum matured organizations for that.

Depending on the selected Agile framework, different organizations call these position different names. As an example, tribe leaders hold similar responsibilities in the Spotify framework. With many years of experience and a very thorough knowledge of SAFe framework, and possibly with Advanced Scrum Master certification and Release Train Engineer Certification, you could aspire to be a Release Train Engineer in the SAFepractised organization.

Solution Train Engineer (STE)

If you have been practising SAFe at RTE level for few years and mastered the art of doing the PI planning and running multiple release trains, the next possible level may be the Solution Train Engineer (STE). However, such a role at a solution or strategic theme level is much more than just a chief scrum master. Read about the Solution Train Engineer at the Scaled Framework site.

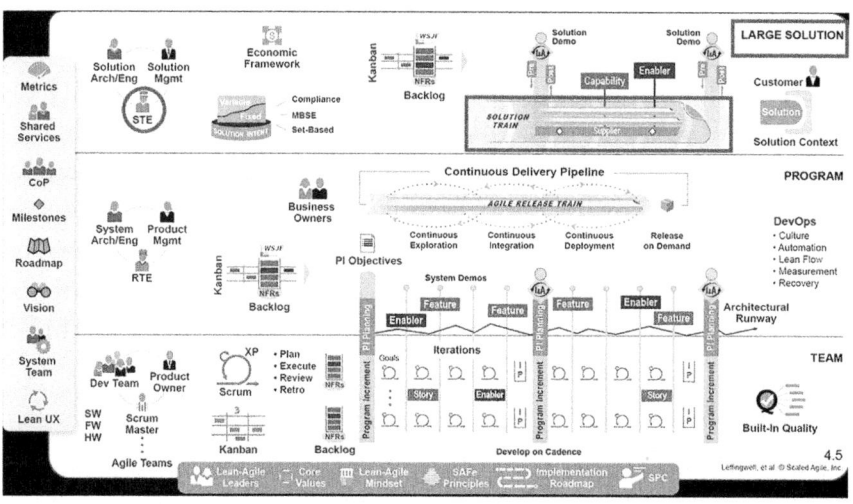

Figure 42: STE as per SAFe framework (Scaleagileframework.com)

Agile transformation Leader/Manager

Many organizations started implementing Agile across organizations, but most got stuck at the scrum of scrum level. How to scale up beyond that point is a puzzle to many organizations. Another point where the hindrance is happening is at the IT organization. Agile is applied to the IT side where the rest of the organization is working in a silo, the traditional way of working. The benefits of Agile cannot be reaped as many do not know how to apply Agile to corporate sections like Human Resources or the Marketing Department.

This is where business agility and Agile transformation come into the picture. That simply means expanding Agile practices into other departments of the organization other than Information Technology.

Agile transformations need to be carefully planned as a strategy. I believe it needs to be run by Agile professionals who have enterprise-level leadership. The key responsibility is an ability to make Agile operational across the organization. Let's call it the Agilecenter of practice (some organizations call this Agile Center or Excellence). You work with Agile professionals and strategic and operational leaders in the organization. This function is important as it provides a base place for all Agile professionals in the organization. They talk differently and they think differently, so a sense of belonging in terms of thought processes is important.

Agile coaching

Agile coaching is another option for career progress. However, the point is to remember that Agile coaching demands a different skill set.

"Agile coaching combines theoretical knowledge, practical experience, and institutional and situational leadership. Ultimately, you should be able to bring out the best in people. It will require your own touch, but you may follow established frameworks such as coactive coaching. "

Lysaa Adkin, a well-known enterprise Agile coach who has a reputation for coaching coaches, explains the Agile coach's job below. Her book *Coaching Agile teams* is a good starting point.

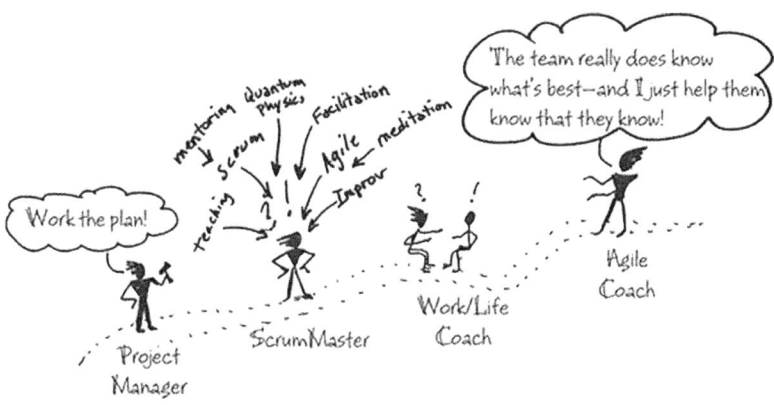

Figure 43 : A possible joruney for Scrum Masters
(Lyssa Adkins' -Coaching Agile Teams)

You can be a team level coach where your main responsibility is coaching the scrum masters, product owners, and the team who are going through the Agile transformation. Your practical experience playing the role of scrum master will come into play in understanding what the team, as well as scrum master, go through, so you can provide practical guidance rather than a formulaic recipe. Understanding context is important when coaching while taking a step away from suggesting solutions.

Enterprise Agile coach

A few years of team level coaching and good practical experience in different frameworks will take you to the possibility of pursuing an enterprise Agile coach position. Most companies have already established this position in their organizational structure either as part of the Agile Center of Excellence or any other form. The difference between a team level coach and enterprise Agile coach is that the enterprise Agile coach is capable of coaching the senior leadership of an organization to go through the cultural and mindset shift. They should be able to match the leadership level discussions and push back and still help everyone understand what is required to adopt Agile at the enterprise level.

Independent consultants

Some people do not like to stick with one organization. Once they build up a good knowledge of Agile and good experience under a good coach, they step out and work as an independent consultant. If you choose that path, you are following the path of most of the Agile practitioners. The good thing about that is that you get to choose what clients, projects, and what duration you want to work with. We see this becoming more and more of a trend, as more and more consultants are following this path.

Summary

I want to highlight that things are changing. Yes, just ten years ago, Agile was hardly a professional career path. But now, with the digital disruption hitting every organization, Agile has become mainstream. The skill set of Agile is highly regarded. There are many paths to choose and even to invent if this is what you are passionate about. While some organizations are a few steps ahead by integrating Agile into the organizational structure, we as Agile professionals must keep educating the rest of the organization to consider it seriously, if they want to be successful in this disruptive world.

END

Printed in Great Britain
by Amazon